TRUTH AND THE PAST

COLUMBIA THEMES IN PHILOSOPHY

COLUMBIA THEMES IN PHILOSOPHY

Editor: **Akeel Bilgrami**, Johnsonian Professor of Philosophy, Columbia University

Columbia Themes in Philosophy is a new series with a broad and accommodating thematic reach as well as an ecumenical approach to the outdated disjunction between analytical and European philosophy. It is committed to an examination of key themes in new and startling ways and to the exploration of new topics in philosophy.

MICHAEL DUMMETT

TRUTH AND THE PAST

COLUMBIA UNIVERSITY PRESS ■ NEW YORK

COLUMBIA UNIVERSITY PRESS

Publishers Since 1893

New York Chichester, West Sussex

Copyright © 2004 Columbia University Press

All rights reserved

Library of Congress Cataloging-in-Publication Data

Dummett, Michael A. E.

Truth and the past / Michael Dummett.

p. cm. — (Columbia themes in philosophy)

Includes bibliographical references and index.

Contents: The concept of truth — The indispensability of the concept of truth — Statements about the past — The semantics of the past tense —The metaphysics of time — Truth: deniers and defenders.

ISBN 0–231–13176–3 (cloth)

1. Truth. 2. Time. I. Title. II. Series.

B1626.D853T78 2004

121—dc21   2003055059

Columbia University Press books are printed on permanent and durable acid-free paper.

Printed in the United States of America

Designed by Lisa Hamm

c 10 9 8 7 6 5 4 3 2 1

CONTENTS

FOREWORD

Michael Dummett's three John Dewey Lectures, bearing the omnibus title "Truth and the Past," were given by him at the Department of Philosophy at Columbia University in the spring semester of 2002. They are presented here in expanded and revised form by Columbia University Press as the inaugural publication of the new series Columbia Themes in Philosophy, with Series Editor Akeel Bilgrami's remarks introducing Dummett on that occasion.

INTRODUCTORY REMARKS

When I arrived as an undergraduate in Oxford in the seventies, philosophers would meet in tournament, as though to break lances in Michael Dummett's honor, especially in the face of what seemed like an invasion of Davidsonian doctrine. To imagine Oxford in those years without Dummett would be to think of eighteenth-century England without Samuel Johnson. There would still have been the Boswells, the Burkes, and the Reynoldses, but no commanding influence. Some years later, I came to the University of Chicago as a graduate student, where Donald

Davidson was presiding, and here Dummett surfaced somewhat differently—in the faded parchment-style photocopies of his William James lectures, which circulated like samizdat writings in Russia. The influence of those lectures has been enormous, and it did not necessarily have to take the form of fetching agreement. Even when they sometimes did not, those writings shaped the interests and the sense of what was important in philosophy for any number of younger philosophers, some of whom are here in the audience today.

Before asking Michael to give his Dewey lectures on the theme of "Truth and the Past," I want to say just a word about something that makes him conspicuously suitable to give a series of lectures which carry the name of John Dewey—his role in the public life of Britain. (You will forgive me, Michael, if, as an Indian, I can't quite get myself to say "*Great* Britain.") In that country he, along with his wife Ann, has written and spoken and served more generally, without fear and without peer, for racial equality. His recent knighthood specifically mentions his contributions in this area in addition to his philosophical work, and I know that that has given him particular pleasure.

Many think of our subject—*analytical* philosophy, as it is called—to be a remote enterprise, with cold characters intricately dissecting concepts. Well, they have not seen the anger well up in Michael Dummett against the racial injustices in British society and its immigration policy, or for that matter against interpretative injustices done to Frege's philosophy of language and mathematics. These are wonderful qualities of temperament for a philosopher to possess, and we all admire him for having done his philosophy as well as lived his public life, not only with great intellectual power but with great intellectual ardor.

———————

Akeel Bilgrami

PREFACE

Chapters 1 to 5 of this book are based on the Dewey Lectures I gave at Columbia University in 2001. The original text of the lectures was published in the *Journal of Philosophy*, vol. C, no. 1, January 2003. I have revised and expanded it, in the process making five chapters out of three lectures. Chapter 6 is separate. It was suggested to me that I add another essay to the text of the lectures, to make the book a more reasonable size. As I had already started writing "Truth: Deniers and Defenders," I used that for the purpose.

As a philosophical topic, truth has been a preoccupation of mine since my earliest days in the subject: I wanted to set out my views, as they now stand, in a comprehensive form. The interpretation of statements about the past, on the other hand, and, more generally, of statements about the temporal, is a topic that has troubled me for several years past. What I have written here is an experiment, much as was my essay of long ago, "The Reality of the Past." I wanted to see if a plausible case could be made, on a justificationist basis, for repudiating antirealism about the past—the view that statements about the past, if true at all, must be true in virtue of the traces past events have left in the present. That view is repugnant, and, as I think

I showed in that earlier article, it leads to consequences very hard to swallow. The position I have adopted in this book is greatly at variance with those I expressed in my not yet published Gifford Lectures of a few years ago. In those, I did not embrace antirealism about the past: but I did maintain that the body of true statements is cumulative. I have not published those lectures, which it is the normal practice to do, because I was troubled that this view was in error. Now that I am publishing a book expressing a different view, I think I will probably publish the Gifford Lectures as I gave them. I do not think anyone should interpret everything that a philosopher writes as if it was just one chapter in a a book he is writing throughout his life. On the contrary, for me every article and essay is a separate attempt to arrive at the truth, to be judged on its own.

I finished the essay which forms chapter 6 a considerable time before Bernard Williams died. His death greatly saddened me; he had been a friend of mine since we were both undergraduates. The essay is not intended to be an appraisal of his book *Truth and Truthfulness* as a whole; it treats of his views on truth, but alludes to truthfulness only glancingly.

I am grateful to Columbia University for having invited me to give the Dewey Lectures. I am especially grateful to Professor Akeel Bilgrami for so kindly looking after me and entertaining me while I was in New York. And I am grateful to my daughter Susanna for accompanying me and taking much trouble also to look after me.

Michael Dummett
Oxford, May 2003

TRUTH AND THE PAST

1

THE CONCEPT OF TRUTH

The distinction between linguistic utterances and what they express is borne in on us by many common experiences, for instance, that of finding out how to say something in another language, and that of rephrasing something we have said to make it clear to our hearer. What a sentential utterance expresses is a proposition. Is "true" to be taken as predicated primarily of sentences or of propositions? Although a number of type sentences, such as "Eels swim to the Sargasso Sea to mate," qualify as true or as false without relativization to any particular occasion of utterance, it is well known that we cannot regard truth as in general being an attribute of type sentences, if only because these may contain indexical expressions whose reference varies from one utterance to another. We must therefore emend our question to: Is "true" to be taken as primarily predicated of propositions or of linguistic entities of some kind?

What reasons are there for opting for one alternative or the other? Frege was strongly in favor of taking truth to attach to propositions, which he called "thoughts" and regarded as being expressed by sentences, in fact as being the senses of declarative sentences; the same thought can be expressed by sentences in different languages, or, indeed, by different sentences in the same language. More exactly, a thought, for Frege, is the sense of a declarative sentence considered independently of the assertoric force that may be attached to it. It need not be a sentence used on its own to make an assertion, but can be a clause within a more complex sentence; but it must be a sentence that could be used on its own to make an assertion, and thus not one containing a pronoun governed by an expression of generality in some other clause. (It can also be an interrogative sentence used to ask a question demanding the answer "Yes" or "No"—a *Satzfrage*.) A thought, for Frege, is either true or false: it cannot be true on one occasion and false on another. From time to time he somewhat casually acknowledged the occurrence of indexical expressions in some sentences, and was content with saying that in such a case the identity of the speaker or the time of utterance contributed to determining the thought expressed.

Davidson, by contrast, has taken truth as attaching to linguistic items, that is, to actual or hypothetical token sentences. Like Frege, however, he treats indexicality as the only reason, at least within a theory of meaning for a language, why truth cannot be taken as attaching to type sentences: he conceives his token sentences as triples, each with a type sentence, a speaker, and a time as its three terms. The reason for taking truth to be an attribute of linguistic items of some kind is obvious. We must do so if we want to use the notion of truth to explain meaning: whether the meaning of a particular expression or the concept of meaning in general, and whether informally or by means of a systematic theory of meaning for a whole language.

Two things must be accomplished if we are to explain the meaning of a word or sentence *ab initio*: we must explain the concept or proposition that that word or sentence expresses, or at least what it is to grasp that concept or proposition; and we must explain in virtue of what that word or sentence expresses that concept or proposition. Any account purporting to provide a full explanation of what is involved in understanding the word or sentence must cover both these aspects. That is not to say that it must cover them *separately*, first explaining the concept or proposition and then stating in virtue of what the word or sentence expresses that concept or proposition; it will do much better to explain the use of the word, or of the words making up the sentence, in such a way as to make manifest what concept or proposition the word or sentence expresses. Plainly, if the explanation is to be given by appeal to the notion of truth, we shall accomplish only the first part of the task if we take truth as attaching to propositions, for no linguistic expression will then be mentioned. If the *meanings* of linguistic expressions are to be explained in terms of the notion of truth, then truth must be taken as an attribute of linguistic expressions of some kind, and not of nonlinguistic entities such as propositions. To take truth as an attribute of propositions is to take meaning as given antecedently to truth and falsity, since it depends on the meaning of a sentence what proposition it expresses: it is therefore to forswear the project of explaining meaning in terms of truth.

This conclusion does not undermine Frege's practice, however much it is at variance with his repeated declarations that it is of thoughts that truth and falsity are predicated. In his *Grundgesetze der Arithmetik*[1] he proceeds quite differently. He lays down stipulations intended to determine the reference (*Bedeutung*) of every expression, simple or complex, of his formal system. These stipulations make no mention of the senses of these expressions; rather, the notion of sense is explained in terms of them. The *Bedeutung* or reference of a sentence is its truth-value. We may here ignore Frege's special doctrine that truth-values are objects, so that a sentence may be described as a "name of a truth-value," as a numerical term is the name of a number. We ought not to interpret Frege's notion of *Bedeutung* as "denotation"; it is better understood in general as "semantic value"—the contribution an expression makes to determining the truth or falsity of a sentence in which it occurs. Frege's stipulations thus serve to determine the truth-value each formal sentence has: and they do so independently of the notion of sense, and in advance of its being introduced at all. The stipulations lay down, inductively, what the semantic value of each expression is to be; the sense of an expression consists in the way in which these stipulations combine, in accordance with how that expression is made up out of its parts, to determine it as having a certain semantic value. The thought expressed by a sentence therefore consists in the condition, as given by those stipulations, for it to have one or the other truth-value; since it will have the value *false* just in case it does not have the value *true*, we may identify it with the condition for it to have the value *true*. To arrive at this account, it was necessary to take the notion of a sentence's having the value *true* as prior to that of the thought it expresses.

In a formal language such as Frege's the type sentences do not vary in truth-value from one context to another; he dreamed of a language for all purposes which would have that property and so be suited to scientific use. We have no such language. Of what items of natural language should truth and falsity be regarded as attributes? Indexicality is far from being the only bar to treating truth as an attribute of type sentences: for one thing, the references of demonstrative expressions are not determined simply by the time of utterance and the identity of the speaker. It is certainly not enough to consider type sentences, together with references associated with their indexical and demonstrative components, as that to which truth-values are attributed. Our objective being to pick out only those forms of words that express definite propositions, we must exclude those that are devoid of truth-value because they do not express any proposition at all. We might try requiring that the sentence be well-formed in the sense that it is grammatically correct in some language, and contains only words that are meaningful in that language and that occur in appropriate contexts. In natural language it is inappropriate to predicate loudness of a chemical substance, so the English sentence "Hydrogen is loud" violates the last condition.

We need, however, to make sure that we pick out only forms of words for which it is determinate in which circumstances what they say may be recognized as true; those, that is, which express quite specific propositions. Plainly, the stipulations we have so far made are insufficient to guarantee that we shall do this. We may try excluding all sentences involving unfamiliar metaphors. A metaphor may be reckoned familiar if it is recorded in dictionaries; but the line between familiar and unfamiliar metaphors is very imprecise (different dictionaries might give different results). We might also exclude all ambiguity, ruling out sentences ambiguous in construction or containing ambiguous words. But this would go too far. In certain contexts no competent speaker would understand an utterance in more than one of the senses it could in principle bear. Can we not recognize this fact by suitably relaxing our ban on ambiguous sentences? A similar problem relates to vagueness. We certainly cannot exclude all sentences containing vague expressions without ruling out the great majority of sentences of the language. Often we can pronounce a statement to be certainly true or certainly false despite the presence in it of vague expressions: we should like to exclude only those whose truth or falsity in given circumstances vagueness would be an obstacle to judging. A particular variety of vagueness is provided by predicates that have a quite determinate theoretical application, but are frequently, and quite legitimately, used in a much looser sense: an excellent example of Peter Unger, adopted by the late David Lewis, is the adjective "flat."[2] It depends on the context how a statement involving the word "flat" is to be understood.

The feature of the context on which it depends is the kind of thing that is being spoken of. A flat terrain is less flat than a bowling green, and less flat yet than a billiard table; we know from what is being spoken of how flat it must be to be rightly said to be flat. Does this make it like other adjectives that admit comparatives? The standard account is that a fat woman is one who is fatter than most women, a large mouse is one that is larger than most mice. Even if correct for these cases, this form of explanation will not do for "flat," since there is such a thing as being absolutely flat, but no such thing as being absolutely fat or absolutely large. I do not know whether a semantic rule can be devised to govern the right way to understand "flat" according to context. It matters little whether such a rule can be formulated: it is implausible that, in interpreting a use of "flat," we actually follow some rule; more likely that, as with an outright ambiguity, we go by how the speaker is likely to have wanted to be understood. In most such cases, the hearer exercises more than his understanding of the words uttered—also his common sense. To know what "flat" means, we must understand "flatter than" and "as flat as," as well as "absolutely flat," and must know that the acceptable application of the word varies with the type of thing of which it is predicated; but there is no need to suppose that we follow any rule laying down appropriate degrees of flatness, even if one could be formulated.

We try, without appealing to the notion of a proposition, to specify linguistic forms that express determinate propositions; and we stumble over one difficulty after another. How, then, can we ever have arrived at the idea that propositions (thoughts in Frege's terminology) are determinately either true or false? We arrive at it because we grasp the notion of understanding a given utterance in a particular way. Most of the features we have been discussing have to do with the way in which a statement will be understood: not with a grasp of all its possible meanings, according to the senses of the words in the language, but with the way in which it is taken when it is made on a particular occasion. The hearer will ignore one possible meaning of a sentence that is in principle ambiguous in favor of another. He will treat the word "flat" as applicable in a manner that accords with what it is applied to. He may correctly construe an unusual turn of phrase as readily as if it were a standard idiom. In short, he will put a particular *interpretation* on it. Sometimes he will need to reflect in order to hit on the meaning the speaker probably intends; more often, he will adopt an interpretation without thinking or striving to attain it.

Aber nicht im Sinne Davidsons: this is not the sense of "interpretation" that figures in Davidson's account of linguistic communication.[3] A Davidsonian interpreter fashions an entire theory of meaning for the speaker's language; but we are concerned with the understanding of a particular utterance in a language known to both speaker and hearer. The senses of the words of a natural language are extremely flexible. When we put them together in a sentence, these senses are greatly stiffened by the presence of the other words; they are stiffened still more by the whole context in which the sentence is uttered. Successful communication depends on its being our habitual practice to adopt that way of construing the utterance of a declarative sentence that renders it as determinate as possible which circumstances will warrant its being judged true and which its being judged false: in other words, as expressing a definite thought, in Frege's sense of "thought." We normally do this automatically, without having to review the different interpretations which the language would admit as possible. It is through our familiarity with this process that we come to grasp the concept of a thought or proposition.

It is impossible to specify those utterances of declarative sentences that express determinate thoughts purely by their linguistic form: we have to take account of how such utterances will be understood. We need to concern ourselves, not with how an utterance may be understood by an individual hearer, who may misunderstand in a variety of ways, but how it will be understood by the great majority of hearers competent in the language. It will be suggested that we should allow for this by conceiving of any statement as being made in a specific context. There is, however, no way to circumscribe the relevant features of the context, and no rule determining from the context, however widely conceived, how the statement will be understood by almost everyone. To know how an ambiguous statement is to be understood often requires a knowledge of what the speaker was likely to be saying; to know what a speaker meant by "flat," one will need to know how close an approximation to absolute flatness would be appropriate in the circumstances. We are forced to consider statements, not as mere concatenations of words, but as subject to particular ways of understanding them, that is, as expressing specific thoughts or propositions. This is the ground for following Frege in regarding truth as attaching, not to linguistic items such as sentences, but to thoughts.

We appear thus to have good reasons to take truth to be attributable to sentences, and good reasons to take it to be attributable to propositions. The choice between sentences and propositions as bearers of truth-values is a false one, however: we should see truth as attaching to a token sentence, but one considered under a particular interpretation. The language determines what interpretations are in principle possible; when the interpretation that is to be put upon the sentence is obvious, it is the circumstances that determine which interpretation that is. The interpretation will select, for each word, one of the senses that the language allows it to bear; it will fix suitable ranges of application for vague expressions involved. The sentence so interpreted will probably not have a truth-value in every imaginable situation; with luck, it will have one in every situation that actually arises. It will therefore not express a thought according to Frege's strict criteria; but we may take it as expressing a proposition that can legitimately be said to be true or false.

BY FAR the most popular type among theories of meaning is the truth-conditional variety. The central tenet of such theories is that the meaning of a statement is given by, or consists in, the condition for it to be true. This needs supplementation by an account of how the meanings of nondeclarative sentences are to be explained by reference to the meanings of correlative statements; but although this supplementation is not unproblematic, we may pass by the question how it is to be provided. The thesis also needs qualification, in that it applies, if at all, only to the central aspect of an expression's meaning which Frege called its "sense" (*Sinn*), and not to those aspects which do not affect the truth or falsity of what is said, such as that which differentiates the words "dead" and "deceased."

It was Frege who first clearly formulated the truth-conditional account of meaning, which was then adopted by Wittgenstein in the *Tractatus*. In Frege the theory has two layers. Each component of a statement has a semantic value, in accordance with its logical category: the semantic value of a singular term is an object, that of a functional expression a function, and so on. It is in virtue of its semantic value that an expression contributes to determining, of any statement containing it, whether or not it is true; according to Frege, the semantic value of a whole sentence is its truth-value, since it is, according to him, in virtue of its truth-value alone that it contributes to determining that of another sentence of which it is a subsentence.

But our understanding of an expression, including a sentence, never consists simply in a grasp of its semantic value. As Kant said, every object is given to us in a particular way. Otherwise expressed, an item of knowledge that someone has can never be completely described by saying that he knows, of some particular object, that such-and-such holds good of it (e.g., that it is what some term refers to). Likewise, when coextensive properties are identified, no item of knowledge can be completely described by saying that someone knows, of a certain property, that something holds good of it (e.g., that some things lack it). Quite evidently, every property that we can ascribe to objects must be given to us in a particular way; and the same applies to every relation and function of which we can speak. For Frege, the sense of an expression is the way its semantic value is given to us in virtue of our understanding of the expression; and this must be a feature of the language, rather than of any one individual's grasp of that expression, since otherwise we should have no common basis for judging whether a statement involving the expression was correct.

There are, as we noted, two parts to knowing what a word or sentence means: we have to grasp the concept or proposition it expresses; and we have to know that that *is* the concept or proposition it expresses. Any account purporting to provide a full explanation of the meaning of the word or sentence must cover both these aspects. There are two opposite errors which reduce an explanation of meaning to only one of its two components. The proponents of what are known as modest theories of meaning maintain that it is no business of a theory of meaning to explain the concepts expressed by the words of a language, but only to specify which concepts they express: they thus dispense with Frege's second layer. Plainly, there can be no theory which could convey to someone ignorant of them all the concepts expressible in a given language by individual words, since it would be necessary to grasp the concepts employed by the theory. Such a theory might well be able to convey many of those concepts; for every other concept expressible in the language, it must be able to explain what is needed for someone to be truly said to grasp that concept, namely by describing the use that he must make of a word that expresses it. A theory that fails to do this will omit an essential ingredient of the understanding of such a word.

The opposite error is most likely to be made in application to whole sentences, and it is usually advanced by those who display an insouciant attitude to quotation marks. The notion of truth, they argue, is needed only to state the *general* principle that to know the content of a proposition is to know the condition for it to be true.

In any particular application of the principle the notion of truth is redundant: to know what "Swans sing before they die" means is to know the condition that must hold good for swans to sing before they die. This thesis is plausible only as an explanation of what it is to know the content of a proposition, not as a complete explanation of what it is to understand a linguistic utterance. Hilary Putnam and the late Elizabeth Anscombe have both suggested that we ought to repudiate the whole distinction between sentences and propositions. They observe quite truly that, in conversing or reading in our own languages, or any others that we know well, we do not normally carry out two successive activities: first that of listening to a sequence of sounds or looking at a string of marks on paper, then that of interpreting them. Rather, as Edmund Husserl insisted,[4] we hear or read the words *as* saying whatever it is that they say; only by a heroic effort can we hear them as mere sounds or see them as mere shapes. We perceive the meaning *in* the words. In the same way, when we are traveling in a country whose language we do *not* know, but which uses the Roman script with which we are familiar, we cannot help reading words and names which we see written up as being pronounced in a certain way, although we know that the natives' pronunciation may be quite different. But the psychological fusion of spelling and sound does not obliterate either the distinction between them or our ability to separate them in thought; likewise, the psychological fusion of verbal form and sense does not obliterate either the distinction between *them* or our ability to separate them in thought. The distinction between the linguistic vehicle and the proposition it is used to express is not to be repudiated on phenomenological grounds such as these.

The argument that the notion of truth is needed only to state a general thesis is plausible only when we have in mind an inquiry into the meaning of a sentence of a given language that is to be answered in that language. If someone, reading a book, asks me, "What does 'fratricide' mean?", I might reply, "To commit fratricide is to kill one's brother": my reply does not refer to the word "fratricide," but only uses it. You could not, however, explain in English what the Chinese or Arabic term for "fratricide" means without mentioning that term. Likewise, to know the condition that must hold good for swans to sing before they die is only one of the things I must know in order to know what "Swans sing before they die" means. No one can explain in full what it is to know the meaning of a particular sentence without referring to that sentence, nor what it is in general to understand a sentence without mentioning sentences. Hence, if the explanation is to involve the notion of truth, truth must be treated as an attribute of a sentence, even if of a sentence under a particular interpretation, rather than just of the proposition it expresses when so interpreted. To explain the content of any particular proposition, such as that swans sing before they die, we may be able to dispense with the notion of truth. But in order to explain in a parallel way the meaning of the *sentence* "Swans sing before they die," we cannot dispense with the notion of truth, even in the particular application. For a truth-conditional theory of *meaning*, the notion of truth is indispensable.

Truth is an attribute of propositions, or, better, of token sentences under particular interpretations. As we saw, there is no way in which to describe the "context" of an utterance fully enough to select a unique interpretation to be put on it. The best a theory of meaning for a whole language can do is to explain the range of possible interpretations of a given type sentence uttered on a specific occasion, with the constraints imposed by our uses of indexicals, pronouns, noun phrases with the definite article, vague expressions, and so on. Each such interpretation will determine a condition for the truth of what is said, so understood. That is the notion of truth with which a truth-conditional theory of meaning must operate.

THE TENDENCY is widespread among philosophers to regard as inviolable the two principles of what, following Quine's terminology, may be labeled semantic shift.[5] The principle of semantic ascent is conventionally illustrated by the conditional

If snow is white, then the statement "Snow is white" is true.

Its twin, the principle of semantic descent, is illustrated by the converse conditional

If the statement "Snow is white" is true, then snow is white.

It is clear how the principles are to be applied to other cases. Some prefer to formulate the principles of semantic shift as applying, not to sentences or statements, but to the propositions they express. The principles then appear in the form

If snow is white, then the proposition that snow is white is true.

and its converse. Frege, like many other philosophers, took a belief to be an attitude to a proposition or thought. He concluded that, in a sentence such as "Edmund believes that Venus has no satellites," the clause "that Venus has no satellites" denotes a thought. Believing that truth attaches primarily to thoughts rather than to sentences, he ought in consistency to have analyzed the sentence "It is true that Venus has no satellites" in the same way, again taking the substantival clause "that Venus has no satellites" to denote a thought. If we accept this analysis, the two principles of semantic shift, taken as applying to propositions or thoughts, can assume the form

If snow is white, then it is true that snow is white.

and *its* converse. It is in fact dubious that Frege would have accepted this analysis, since he declared that the sentences "Snow is white" and "It is true that snow is white" expressed the very same thought and had the very same sense. He is therefore more likely to have taken the expression "it is true that" to be a sentential operator carrying any sentence into one with the same truth-value, in which case the foregoing conditional and its converse would involve no semantic shift whatever.

The principles of semantic shift are very far from being inviolable. The quickest way to see this is to consider the semantic paradoxes concerning truth such as the Liar, asking not to which statements of natural language the predicate "true" can be correctly applied, but what status can consistently be assigned to the paradoxical utterances. It is not enough simply to declare them to be neither true nor false, even if such a declaration is sound, since paradoxes can be generated without tangling with the notion of falsity at all. A paradox results from having the liar say, "The statement I am now making is not true"; following Curry, we can generate a paradox without the use of negation by having someone other than the pope say, "If the statement I am now making is true, I am the pope." One suggestion is that by means of such a paradoxical utterance the speaker fails to make any statement, and that therefore, in using the definite description "the statement I am now making," he is failing to refer to anything. But this, as a strategy for devising a consistent description of all these cases, fails if we have the liar say, "I am now making no true statement." Perhaps it may be allowed that the speakers in these cases do make statements, but proposed that the predicate "true" can no more be appropriately applied to these statements than the predicate "loud" can be appropriately applied to chemical substances. This does not resolve our difficulties, either. It may be held that there are numbers to which the predicate "positive" cannot be appropriately applied, for instance complex numbers such as i, the square root of -1; but that does not forbid us to make general statements about positive numbers, including the statement "A negative number has no positive square root." There is nothing for it but to deny that, in application to the paradoxical utterances, the principles of semantic shift fail to hold good. A speaker who said, "I am now making no true statement," was not then making any true statement; but we cannot, by invoking the principle of semantic ascent, infer from that fact that he *was* making a true statement.

Undoubtedly, the principles of semantic shift can be used to explain many occurrences of the word "true" in everyday discourse. In particular, certain intuitively valid but semantically puzzling inferences may be shown to be valid when principles of semantic ascent are added to their premises. Examples are:

> Edmund said, "Bears like honey."
> Bears do like honey.
> So Edmund made a true statement.

and:

> Edwina believes that bears like honey.
> Bears do like honey.
> So Edwina has a true belief.

The addition of the relevant principles of semantic ascent makes these inferences unproblematic (provided, in the second case, that we take a "that"-clause after "believes" or "it is true" as denoting a proposition); but principles of semantic shift themselves remain perplexing. Syntactically, of course, they are not puzzling at all: it is easy to specify their general form syntactically. In semantic terms, however, they are difficult to explain. These are general *principles*, that is, principles to the effect that all—better, most—conditionals of a certain form hold good. Normally, instances of such very general principles hold good in virtue of the denotations or semantic values of the expressions involved, rather than their specific meanings. But what, in these cases, is the connection between the semantic values of the expressions occurring in the antecedent and the consequent? In one clause reference is made to a statement or to a proposition; the other need contain no mention of statements or propositions, but only of snow, the planet Venus, bears, or anything else whatever of which nothing is said in the former clause. Well, how is it with sentences of the general form, "'Hillary Clinton' is the name of Hillary Clinton," "'Milan' is the name of Milan," and so forth? Here we also have semantic shift. Admittedly, not every statement of this form is correct: not, for instance, "'The pope' is the name of the pope." We have to ensure that the expression cited *is* a name. But then we equally have to avoid such misbegotten instances of semantic ascent as "If the objection was overruled, then the judge's statement, 'The objection is overruled,' was true." Are we entitled to ask what is the connection between the denotation of the expression "'Hillary Clinton'" and that of the expression "Hillary Clinton"? The answer, "The former is the name of the latter," does not give an answer of the kind we want; it is essential to the general form illustrated by these sentences that it is by means of the former, that is, the name, that we are picking out the latter, the person.

It is an essential feature of linguistic exchange that we do not merely apprehend the meaning of what is said but are aware of the words used to say it. The opposite can be imagined. After all, we often remember the content of what someone said without remembering the words that were used; we can therefore fantasize our always being unaware of anyone's actual words, including our own, but only their content. In such conditions, we should not always know whether a person or place had been referred to by name or by some equivalent means, or even have the concept of a name that we have now: we could not even frame such a sentence as "'Milan' is the name of Milan." The apparently puzzling character of conditionals instantiating principles of semantic shift, such as "If snow is white, then the proposition that snow is white is true," arises from the use of semantic theories which divorce the semantic value of an expression from its meaning—of what Frege called its *Bedeutung* from its *Sinn*—as well as from its phonetic and orthographic character. Such semantic theories do less than justice to how we apprehend utterances. In a semantic theory of this kind the connective "if . . . then" may be explained by the two-valued truth-table, which takes into account only the truth-values of the two clauses. If we explain it in a way that takes account of the propositions expressed by the clauses, the difficulty vanishes. If, for instance, we stipulate that an indicative conditional may be asserted if a willingness to assert the proposition expressed by the antecedent will carry with it an at least equal willingness to assert that expressed by the consequent, there will be no problem in characterizing the general form of these semantic shifts, namely by stating the obvious fact that the proposition expressed by one clause is that referred to in the other: it is only the delusion that we must give the explanation solely in terms of semantic value—of what is referred to—and not in terms of how we refer to it that causes us perplexity.

This is not to question the validity or utility of the distinction between sense and reference, or meaning and semantic value. It is only to say that if we admit the notions of the proposition expressed by a statement and of the senses of the words and phrases that compose it, we may legitimately use these notions for various semantic purposes: to characterize certain general forms of statement; to explain the meanings of certain logical constants and certain sentence-forming operations; and to analyze the validity of certain forms of inference. To demand that such purposes should be carried out by appeal only to the semantic values of the expressions involved is to make unnecessarily heavy weather of these tasks.

NOW THE general belief that the principles of semantic shift are inviolable has had two conflicting consequences. One is the strong appeal of the minimalist attitude to the concept of truth. The other is the widespread acceptance of truth-conditional theories of meaning. The minimalist thesis is twofold: (1) that every instance—or almost every instance—of the principles of semantic shift, either as applied to statements or as applied to propositions, holds good; and (2) that by stipulating that all those instances hold good which in fact do so, we give the *whole* explanation of the meaning of the word "true." Both minimalist conceptions of truth and truth-conditional theories of meaning derive their attraction from a common source; but they are incompatible with each other. Minimalism conflicts with a truth-conditional theory of meaning because it assumes meaning as given antecedently to the notion of truth. This is most obvious for that version of minimalism which regards truth as primarily an attribute of propositions. What proposition is expressed by a statement depends upon that aspect of the statement's meaning that Frege called its "sense": obviously, you cannot know what proposition a statement expresses unless you know what it means. The notion of the meaning of a statement is thus prior to that of a proposition; and a minimalist of this variety is taking the notion of a proposition as prior to the notion of truth. But a truth-conditional theory of meaning explains meaning in terms of truth, and thus takes truth as prior to meaning. The two theories are thus irreconcilable.

Let us look at this in more detail. The minimalist stipulates, by some means, instances of semantic ascent, such as

> If swans sing before they die, then the proposition that swans sing before they die is true.

and instances of semantic descent, such as

> If the proposition that swans sing before they die is true, then swans sing before they die.

The truth-conditional theorist may lay down that the sense of a statement in the language for which he is giving a theory of meaning is the condition for it to express a true proposition. Suppose that that language is Arabic. How is the theory to determine which proposition is expressed by the Arabic translation of the sentence "Swans sing before they die"? What other criterion can the theorist adopt, if he is to be faithful to his truth-conditionalist principles, than that it expresses that proposition the condition for whose truth coincides with the condition for the truth of the sentence? So he cannot avoid using "true" as applying to sentences as well as to propositions. Therefore, in order to identify the proposition expressed by the Arabic sentence in question, he will have to be able to derive from his theory of meaning that the condition for its truth is that swans sing before they die. Hence, while he might be prepared to concede that, collectively, the minimalist's principles of semantic shift account for the notion of truth as applied to propositions, he needs in addition a notion of truth as applied to sentences (if necessary, under some interpretation) in order to determine which proposition each sentence, thus interpreted, expresses; and this notion, being prior to that of a proposition and of the meaning of a sentence, he cannot derive from the principles of semantic shift as enunciated by a minimalist of this variety.

The minimalist cannot take the same route, however. It will do him no good to choose to stipulate the principles of semantic shift as applied to sentences or statements as well as to propositions, and then to invoke the truth-conditional criterion to determine the proposition expressed by the statement "Swans sing before they die": that will not help him at all to determine what proposition is expressed by the translation of that statement into Arabic.

But would not that strategy work if the language in question were not Arabic but English? What is special about English is that we are taking it as the metalanguage of the truth-conditional theory of meaning and as the language in which instances of the principles of semantic shift are framed. A stipulation of those principles, as applied to sentences, takes the meanings of those sentences as already given. This is in part because, in order to derive from those principles an understanding, whether complete or partial, of the meaning of the word "true," it is not enough to know, for example, that the statement: .

> If swans sing before they die, then the statement "Swans sing before they die" is true.

and its converse both hold good: one must grasp and accept the propositions expressed by those statements, which is to say that one must *understand* the two statements. But since the sentence "Swans sing before they die" is not only referred to but occurs as a clause in both statements, this means that one must understand that sentence. But that is not all. In order to recognize a conditional statement *as* an instance of one of the principles of semantic shift, you must be able to recognize that the proposition expressed in one clause is the same as that expressed by the statement referred to in the other; you must therefore understand not only the former clause but also the statement referred to in the other clause. It may be objected that it is enough to notice that the same form of words is used in one clause and mentioned in the other (with due allowance for changes of pronouns, tenses, etc.). But it is *not* enough. To borrow an excellent example of Elizabeth Anscombe's,[6] the conditional

> If Henry can eat any fish, then the statement "Henry can eat any fish" is true.

is *not* an instance of the principle of semantic ascent. Henry can eat trout; it does not follow at all that it is true to say, "Henry can eat any fish."

Thus by stipulating the principles of semantic shift, as expressed in English, the minimalist takes as given the meanings of English statements. He is claiming, by means of that stipulation, to give a comprehensive account of the meaning of the word "true" as applied to statements made in English. He must therefore have found some means, adequate in his eyes, for specifying the meanings of such statements; or else he is simply trading upon his readers' already knowing the English language. It follows that he cannot accept the proposal that the meanings of statements, whether of English or of any other language, are to be specified by laying down the conditions for them to be true, in that sense of "true" of which the minimalist claims to have given an account. For statements made in English, such a procedure would be grossly circular; and the minimalist has given no account of the meaning of "true" as applied to statements made in any other language.

But can we not get round the difficulty by means of a stipulation that takes no account of the phenomenon of semantic shift, but nevertheless yields all the instances of the principles governing it? Such a stipulation is that embodied in a Tarskian truth-definition, adapted to natural language, with the semantic paradoxes avoided by some suitable means (say by Kripke's construction). The truth-definition itself does not recognize or appeal to the occurrence of semantic shift: a recognition of it takes place only in the surrounding patter stating the alleged condition for the adequacy of the definition. The definition simply yields, for each statement of the language, what is known as a T-sentence, namely a biconditional incorporating, for that statement, the principles of semantic ascent and descent, without acknowledging that that is what each such biconditional is.

A truth-definition for a language aims, of course, at defining the predicate "true" as applied to statements of that language. Like all definitions, it takes the language in which it is expressed, save for the term being defined, as understood; and if that language coincides with or is an extension of the object-language, it takes the object-language as understood. So, although we have circumvented recognition of instances of semantic shift as such, we still have our first reason for attributing to one who stipulates that such instances are to hold good the assumption of a prior understanding of the language, namely that the clauses of the T-sentences must be understood if the definition is to be understood.

Donald Davidson is well known for having proposed that a Tarskian truth-definition for a natural language be turned on its head to provide a truth-conditional theory of meaning for that language. By "turning it on its head" he had in mind that, instead of taking meaning as given in order to explain the notion of truth, we should take the notion of truth as given and use it to explain meaning. To take the notion of truth as given is to know about it whatever has to be known in order to see a Davidsonian truth-theory of this kind as a theory *of meaning*, that is, as specifying the meanings of the words and sentences of the language. The word "true," as used in the truth-theory, could not be replaced by some arbitrary nonsense word: it is not a theoretical term that derives its whole content from its role in the theory. We have to bring to the theory our intuitive understanding of the word "true." The theory, as stated in Davidson's classic papers, does not seek to make explicit in what this intuitive understanding consists, or to spell out the connection between truth-conditions and meaning.

Now could the meaning of the word "true," as used in a Davidsonian theory of meaning. be given in the way that the minimalist favors, namely by stipulating that all legitimate instances of the principles of semantic shift are to hold good? To avoid difficulties about how such instances are recognized, let us suppose that the stipulation is effected by a Tarskian truth-definition. That, according to the minimalist, tells us what "true" means. We have now to use this term to specify the meanings of the words and sentences of the language. To do this, following Davidson's recipe, we simply repeat the truth-definition all over again, with the only difference that we no longer call it a *definition*, but a *theory*; what were clauses of the definition have now become postulates of the theory. The procedure is manifestly ludicrous. A minimalist account of truth rules out a truth-conditional account of meaning.

BUT SHOULD meaning be explained truth-conditionally? Wittgenstein thought, or at least frequently wrote as if he thought, that the meaning of a word or type sentence is constituted by its use, that is, the manner in which it is (correctly) employed in linguistic interchange (spoken or written). On the face of it, this seems undeniable. How else do we tell whether or not someone has mastered a language than by attending to the use he makes of its words and sentences—observing what he says when using that language, how he responds when someone speaks in that language to him, and other features of his associated behavior? If we want to engage in what Davidson calls radical interpretation—trying to understand the speakers of a language unassisted by any bilingual interpreter, phrase book, or dictionary—what else is there to go on but the use the speakers make of its words and sentences?

What constitutes "use"? There are forms of sentence which are commonly used to express something different from what their composition would suggest; this is particularly true of tautologies such as "Boys will be boys," "What is done is done," "Either she is your sister or she is not." One must know these usages in order to speak the language successfully; but they illustrate only a peripheral feature of use. In Wittgenstein's writings, there are three fundamental features of use. First is what is accepted as justifying an utterance. If the utterance is of an assertoric character, this becomes what vindicates it or establishes it as correct. This comes under the head of the *grounds* for asserting a statement: these include what is acknowledged as entitling a speaker to make the assertion, what requires him to withdraw it, and in what circumstances, if any, it is conclusively shown to be correct.

The second feature consists of what a speaker commits himself to by saying something, and what is counted as a proper response to another's utterance. When the utterance is assertoric, this comes under the head of the *consequences* of making the assertion: what actual or potential difference it makes to what is done or said by the speaker or his hearers. It includes what constitutes acting on an assertion when it is accepted, as well as inferences drawn from the statement so asserted.

The third feature is a more reflective one, namely the point of having a given form of words in the language. To ask after its point is to ask what we are able to do with that form of words that we could not do without it. Often there will be little reason to ask such a question—the point of having a given form of words may be obvious. But it may seem worthwhile to inquire, for instance, what is the point of having such a form of sentence as counterfactual conditionals, and right to criticize some account of their meanings on the ground that it deprives them of any point. But, although a question of the form, "What is the point of having such-and-such a form of words in the language?" is often philosophically useful to ask, it is arguable that this is not a genuinely independent feature of use: a fully adequate account of the use of a given form of sentence will always *show* what is the point of having it in the language, whenever there really is a point in this.

None of these features of a language involves the conception of a statement's *being* true. The first two of them, when applied to the making of statements, may be said to be concerned with notions that involve truth: that of establishing something as true and that of acting on the truth of something. So could we explain meaning in terms of one or other of these notions, or perhaps of both of them together? By far the most systematic attempt to do so, although only for a restricted segment of language, is the intuitionistic theory of meaning for mathematical statements. In this, the meaning of a mathematical statement is not explained in terms of the condition for it to be true, independently of our knowledge. It is explained, rather, in terms of what is required of a proof of that statement. A proof is what is needed in order to warrant the assertion of a mathematical statement; the intuitionist account of meaning thus explains the statement in terms of the first of the three foregoing features of its use. The consequences of accepting a mathematical statement as true are that we can use it to make inferences that lead to proofs of further statements. If we know the meanings of all other mathematical statements, as given in these terms, we shall also know what is required for drawing a conclusion from any given statement; so we do not need a separate specification of the second feature of its use.

It is plausible that this latter point can be generalized. Wittgenstein, engaged in informal discussions of one or another form of words, sometimes concentrates on one of the two fundamental features of use, sometimes on the other, sometimes on both of them simultaneously. But when we are aiming at sketching the form that a systematic theory of meaning for a whole language ought to take, and are aiming to formulate the theory directly in terms of one or more features of the use of statements of that language, it is plausible that we may frame it in terms of just one of the two fundamental features of use, just as the intuitionist theory of meaning for mathematical statements is framed in terms of what is needed for the proof of a given statement, and not also in terms of what could be proved from it. This is because it is a requirement upon a language that functions as a language ought that there be harmony between the two features of use: that is, that we draw from a statement only consequences that match the grounds for asserting or accepting it, and that we accept it on any grounds that justify the consequences we draw from it. If such harmony prevails, then one of the two fundamental features of use will be derivable from the other, and the meanings of individual words and sentences of the language can be given in terms of either such feature. A theory of meaning given in terms of the grounds for asserting a statement I shall call a *justificationist* theory; one given in terms of the consequences of accepting a statement I shall call a *pragmatic* theory. The intuitionist theory is a justificationist theory of meaning for mathematical statements.

There is indeed no guarantee that the linguistic practices accepted by the speakers of any actual language will conform to the requirements of harmony, any more than they will satisfy the requirement that there be no ambiguity. But, if they do not, those practices are in need of reform. A theory of meaning for a language in need of reform will probably be imperfectly coherent, and will in any case be of minor value. If the best fully coherent theory of meaning for a language fails to fit completely with the conventional practices of its speakers, the language is in need of reform; and the theory will show in which respects it needs to be reformed.

A proponent of a truth-conditional theory of meaning is not aiming to give a stipulative definition of "meaning": he is not just laying down that, for him, the meaning of a statement is constituted by the condition for it to be true. If he were, his thesis would be trivial. Rather, he is aiming to *explain* what meaning consists in. Now what anyone needs to know in order to be able to engage in the communal practice of speaking and writing a particular language is the use that is made, by those who know it, of its expressions and sentences; and, as already remarked, the criterion for his knowing the language is that he manifests such knowledge. The truth-conditional theorist therefore has two challenges to meet. He has, first, to show how the fundamental features of the use of any statement of the language can be derived from the conditions for its truth: how we can from these conditions determine what are the grounds for asserting the statement, and how accepting it will affect the actions of a speaker or hearer. In showing this, the theorist will be spelling out that connection between the use of a language and the truth-conditions of its statements—the connection between truth and meaning—that Davidson, in his original formulations, left as tacitly understood. Until he has done this, the truth-conditional theorist will not yet have vindicated his claim that his theory of truth-conditions constitutes a theory *of meaning*. To vindicate it, he admittedly need not derive all aspects of the use of a statement: he may put some down to particular linguistic conventions. For instance, he may reasonably hold that there are conventions governing entitlement to assert statements of different forms, conventions that do not affect the meanings of those statements. We do not regard it as proper to assert a mathematical statement unless it has been proved; otherwise it can only be conjectured. We can easily imagine, however, people who regard it as legitimate to assert such a statement when there is a probable ground, falling short of proof, for conjecturing its truth, even though they have the same standards of proof as we do and are as interested in discovering proofs: they would mean the same by their mathematical statements as we mean by them. But the theorist must be able to determine from the condition for the truth of any statement what—if anything—counts as *conclusively* establishing it.

By meeting this first challenge the truth-conditional theorist will have shown that his theory is truly a theory of meaning, but he will not have shown that a theory of meaning must necessarily assume a truth-conditional form. After all, if the criterion for knowing a language is that a subject manifests a knowledge of the use of its expressions and sentences, will not the most direct theory of meaning for that language be a straightforward (though of course very complex) description of how the language functions, that is, an account of the use of its words and sentences? Why do we need a digression via the truth-conditions of its statements, even if this eventually yields the account of use that we are after? To demonstrate the necessity of a truth-conditional theory of meaning, a proponent of such a theory must argue that use cannot be described without appeal to the conditions for the truth of statements; insofar as he is aiming to explain understanding as well as meaning, as he ought to be aiming to do, he must claim that anyone who has mastered the use of expressions of a language must have acquired an implicit grasp of the concept of truth and an implicit conception of the conditions for the truth of its statements. It will then follow that a theory of meaning in terms of use must be a truth-conditional theory.

2

THE INDISPENSABILITY OF
THE CONCEPT OF TRUTH

The first chapter ended by claiming that the proponent of a truth-conditional theory of meaning must argue that use cannot be described without appeal to the conditions for the truth of statements, and that anyone who has mastered the use of expressions of a language must have acquired an implicit grasp of the concept of truth. To an important degree, such an argument would be correct. It was maintained that an adequate theory of meaning must yield an account of what difference the assertion of a statement makes, actually or potentially, to what subsequently happens. This includes the difference that acceptance of the statement by a hearer makes to what he subsequently thinks, says, and does. But what, in general, does accepting some statement as true involve? We do not merely react piecemeal to what other people say to us: we use the information we acquire, by our own observation and inferences and by what we are told, in speech and writing, by others, to build up an integrated picture of the world. To take a statement as contributing to this picture of the world, that is, of reality independent of our will, is to take it as true. So the practice of using language in which we learn to engage does impart to us an implicit grasp of the concept of truth.

The intuitionist account of the meaning of mathematical statements does not employ the notion of a statement's being true, but only that of something's being a proof of the statement. It is therefore natural to conclude that a justificationist theory of meaning can altogether dispense with the notion of truth—that is, of a statement's *being* true, as opposed to its being recognized or accepted as true; presumably the same will apply to a pragmatist theory of meaning. This is a mistake, however. That part of the intuitionist theory that specifies the meanings of particular expressions uses the notion of proof, but not the notion of truth; but, as an overall theory of meaning for mathematical statements, it needs a notion of truth. This is for two reasons, which apply to any theory of meaning whatever.

If Frege's account of sense is right, as I believe, then the theory of sense rests upon a semantic theory as base. Frege explained the sense of an expression as the way in which its semantic value is given to us. His semantic theory was a classical two-valued one, so, for him, the semantic value of an expression was its contribution to determining the truth-value of a sentence in which it occurred. This agrees with the way in which a semantic theory is usually characterized—it explains how the truth-value of a sentence is determined in accordance with its composition. But many theories of meaning do not take a statement's simply being true or not being true as their central notion. The intuitionistic theory takes as its central notion that of a construction's being a proof of a statement—a choice that shrinks the gap between sense and semantic value to the minimum; a theory that rests on the possible-worlds semantics for statements involving modality takes as its central notion that of a statement's being true in a possible world. We must therefore generalize our characterization of a semantic theory. In any theory of meaning, a statement will have what may be called a *fundamental semantic property*, definable in terms of the central notion of the theory. In a possible-worlds theory this will be the property of being true in the possible worlds in some set and not in others; in the intuitionistic theory it is that of being proved by certain constructions and not by others. A semantic theory must then be characterized as one that explains how the fundamental semantic property of any statement is determined in accordance with its composition. We may still hold that, within any theory of meaning, its component theory of sense will rest on the base of a semantic theory, understood in this generalized manner.

Now a comprehensive theory of meaning for any language must aim at giving a complete account of how that language functions. The philosophical purpose of considering the form that a theory of meaning for a particular language should take does not lie in any special interest we might have in that individual language, but is to illuminate the general nature of linguistic meaning: what it is for linguistic utterances to have the significance that they have, and what, therefore, it is to have a language at all and to engage in the practice of speaking it. Hence a theory of meaning for a particular language should be conceived by a philosopher as describing the practice of linguistic interchange by speakers of the language without taking it as already understood what it is to have a language at all: that is what, by imagining such a theory, we are trying to make explicit.

A salient part of using a language is to give arguments in support of some conclusion, either to induce the hearer to accept that conclusion or to justify a prior assertion of it when challenged. Hence a theory of meaning ought, as one of its tasks, to give an account of the procedure of deductive inference, and supply a criterion for the validity of such an inference. It is this purpose that a semantic theory is intended to serve: it explains how the fundamental semantic property of any statement is determined in accordance with its composition in order to characterize valid deductive inferences by reference to this. It is here presupposed that the validity of an inference will always turn solely on the semantic values of the expressions involved; any inference whose validity depends upon their specific senses can be handled by replacing such expressions by equivalents as laid down by their definitions.

A deductive argument is valid if it is guaranteed to transmit some desirable property from premises to conclusion; this property is normally taken to be truth. A theory of meaning, and indeed a semantic theory, thus needs a notion of truth, as that which is guaranteed to be transmitted from premises to conclusion of a deductively valid argument, in addition to the central semantic notion, if that is not already the notion of truth. But the point is more general than that. What is the meaning of a declarative sentence? One answer might be: it is the principle that governs what it serves to convey to a hearer when that sentence is used on its own on any occasion to make an assertion, that is, how the hearer takes things to be if he accepts the assertion as correct. This is indeed an important feature of the meaning of the sentence, and it is how the question what the sentence means is often answered. But it is only one feature of the sentence's meaning: we may call it the *assertoric content* of the sentence. But it plainly does not constitute the whole of what the sentence means. We need to know, in addition, what contribution that sentence makes to the assertoric content of a more complex sentence of which it is a subsentence, and this is not in general determined by its own assertoric content. We may call this second feature the *ingredient sense* of the sentence. Two sentences may have the same assertoric content, but different ingredient senses. Examples may most easily be given by exploiting the phenomenon called "rigidity" by Saul Kripke.[1] The two sentences

It is raining here.

and

It is raining where I am.

have the same assertoric content: if you believe a friend who, speaking to you on the telephone, utters either sentence, you learn exactly the same as if he had uttered the other sentence of the pair. But the sentences do not have the same ingredient senses, as is shown by the quite different meanings (assertoric contents) of the two sentences that result from inserting the quantifier "always":

It is always raining here.

and

It is always raining where I am.

The divergence occurs because the adverb "here" is temporally rigid, while the adverbial phrase "where I am" is temporally flexible. There are examples of a different kind. The sentences

I shall give you a D.

and

I intend to give you a D.

have the same assertoric content; but their ingredient senses differ, since the conditionals

If I give you a D, you will forfeit your grant.

and

If I intend to give you a D, you will forfeit your grant.

have different assertoric contents. (In English, the antecedent of the first conditional is grammatically in the present tense, but its sense is future; in Italian, it would have the same future-tense form as the simple sentence.) Sentences carrying presuppositions provide further examples. The sentences

Clare's husband is Egyptian.

and

Clare is married to an Egyptian.

have the same assertoric content, since a hearer who did not know that Clare was married would learn this as well from hearing the first sentence as from hearing the second. But they do not have the same ingredient sense, since their negations are not equivalent (negation does not cancel presupposition). One way to understand the traditional semantics for many-valued logics, with its distinction between designated and undesignated values, is to take the assertoric content of a sentence to be given by the condition for it to have a designated truth-value, while the distinctions among different undesignated values, and those (if any) among different designated ones, serve to explain the ingredient senses of sentences.

The notion of assertoric content provides a second reason a theory of meaning needs a concept of truth. Central to any description of the practice of using a language is an account of its use to make assertions and of the responses they evoke in their hearers. The description must cover other uses of language, but assertion is primary: questions call for assertions to be made, and it must be possible to say whether a request has been granted or declined, a demand complied with or flouted. It is from the practice of making assertions that the notion of truth first arises: it is of the essence of that practice that assertions can be judged correct or incorrect. We may accordingly take a statement to be true if it would be correct to assert it; more exactly, if an assertion of it would be justified, whether or not a particular speaker would have been justified in making it. This obviously depends on the assertoric content of the sentence used to make the statement, since it relates to the import of that sentence uttered on its own. The property of statements thus characterized coincides with the property guaranteed to be transmitted from premises to conclusion of a valid deductive inference. For what we need to know, of such an inference, is that, if we are entitled to assert the premises, we shall be entitled to assert the conclusion.

The defenders of truth-conditional theories of meaning are thus right to argue that the concept of truth is indispensable. The concept of truth is the pivot about which a theory of meaning is brought to bear on metaphysics. Metaphysics is concerned with the general nature of reality, and, as the opening remarks of the *Tractatus* state,[2] reality is constituted not by the totality of objects that exist but by the totality of facts that obtain. Facts are true propositions: so metaphysics concerns itself with what truths hold good in general. But we can by no means conclude to the correctness of a truth-conditional theory of meaning. We cannot do so for two reasons. First, there is no argument to show that truth needs to be taken as the central notion of the semantic theory underlying a sound theory of meaning. This central notion must be selected in order to explain in terms of it the whole meanings of sentences— not just their assertoric contents, but their ingredient senses; indeed, it is especially concerned with their ingredient senses, since one of the primary functions of a semantic theory is to explain the logical constants.

Secondly, different theories of meaning have different conceptions of truth. It is not enough for the truth-conditional theorist to argue that we need the concept of truth: he must show that we should have the same conception of truth that he has. We need the concept of truth for the two purposes I have stated, but giving these two purposes does not yet say what it is for a statement made by means of a sentence whose meaning has been given in terms of the central notion of the theory to be true. We shall expect that any given theory will explain this—will characterize truth—by reference to its central notion. The result will not in general conform to the principle of bivalence upon which truth-conditional theories of meaning depend, the principle, namely, that every statement devoid of ambiguity and vagueness is determinately either true or false. For instance, the central notion of the intuitionistic theory of meaning for mathematical statements is that of proof; and within that theory the truth of such a statement may be said to consist in the existence of a means, effective in principle, for finding a proof of it. The canons of correct reasoning in intuitionistic mathematics debar us from restricting true statements to those we have actually proved. Thus the semantic theory stipulates that a proof of a disjunctive statement "A or B" must consist of a proof either of A or of B. But we are entitled to assert such a statement even when we do not have a proof of either disjunct, but merely have an effective means in principle of finding a proof of one or the other: for instance, when A is the statement that some large natural number is prime, and B the statement that it is composite. That is the notion of truth appropriate to the intuitionistic theory of meaning. It quite obviously does not respect bivalence.

We are now in a position to evaluate the principles of semantic shift. It follows from what was said about truth and assertoric content that, for any statement A, the assertoric content of A and of the statement "A is true" must be the same. It does not in the least follow that their ingredient senses must coincide. Now the principles of semantic ascent and descent, applied to a statement A, are conditional statements of which A is the antecedent or the consequent. They therefore involve, not merely the assertoric content of A and of "A is true" but also their ingredient senses. We accordingly have no general reason, independent of the particular theory of meaning that we favor, for regarding either of the two principles, or the biconditional T-sentence that combines them, as holding good. Whether they hold good in any particular case depends on our theory of meaning and the conception of truth appropriate to it, as well as on the particular statement to which they are being applied. The widespread obsession with the principles of semantic shift as known to be inviolable in advance of any further inquiry into the concept of truth is utterly misplaced.

Consider the conception of the truth of statements in the future tense according to which they become true or false only at the time to which they relate; or the more sophisticated conception under which determinism is rejected and a future-tense statement is true at a given time only if it holds in all subsequent courses of events causally compatible with how things are and have been up to that time, and false only if it fails in all of them. These conceptions will each accord with the account that its proponent gives of the meanings of sentences in the future tense. Under the first of these conceptions the statement "In 2003 Bush will veto a bill outlawing the death penalty" is neither true nor false now; not being a determinist, I imagine that the same holds good under the second of the two conceptions, too. Now an application of the principle of semantic ascent yields the conditional:

> If in 2003 Bush vetoes a bill outlawing the death penalty, the statement "In 2003 Bush will veto a bill outlawing the death penalty" is true.

By contraposition, this yields:

> If the statement "In 2003 Bush will veto a bill outlawing the death penalty" is not true, then Bush will not in 2003 veto a bill outlawing the death penalty.

Clearly, the proponent of neither of the two conceptions of truth will accept this, nor, accordingly, the principle of semantic ascent as applied to statements in the future tense. If you believe in the principle, you will persuade them to accept it only if you can induce them to repudiate their conceptions of truth, and hence to modify their theories of meaning.

It is because they have correctly perceived that the assertoric contents of the sentences "'Snow is white' is true" or "It is true that snow is white" and of "Snow is white"—what is conveyed to a hearer by means of an assertion of one sentence or the other—must coincide that philosophers have been tempted to regard the principles of semantic shift as inviolable. Frege perceived this. He drew a firm distinction between grasping a proposition (a thought in his terminology) or expressing it and judging it to be true or asserting it, and rather naturally described the transition from the first to the second as an "advance from the thought to the truth-value." One might, therefore, expect the predicate "is true" to effect a linguistic expression of this advance. But it does not. What does so is no predicate at all, but the assertoric force attached to the sentence, signified, in Frege's formal notation, by his assertion sign. That is why Frege said that the words "is true" appear to attempt "to make the impossible possible"—to express by means of a predicate what is not a genuine predicate. But of course they do not really make it possible: by passing from the sentence "Snow is white" to the sentence "It is true that snow is white," we do not go from the expression of a thought to an assertion of its truth: until we have attached assertoric force to the first sentence or to the new one, we are still merely expressing a thought, not asserting it. And so he was led to say that the thought expressed by the new sentence containing the word "true" was the very same as that expressed by the original sentence.

If he had meant no more than that they had the same assertoric content, he would have been right. Unfortunately, he identified the sense of a sentence with the thought it expressed, and so declared the *senses* of the two sentences to be the same. He had some excuse for doing so, in that, in his semantic theory, a sentence—except when it occurs in indirect speech—contributes to the truth-value of a more complex sentence of which it is part solely in virtue of being itself true or not being true, so that its ingredient sense is determined by its assertoric content; but in a more general context, independent of the semantic theory, it is a false conclusion.

Philosophers have a strong intuition that the concepts of truth and meaning are inextricably linked; after all, if one fully grasps the meanings of two statements and can take one to be true without taking the other to be true, those meanings must differ. The intuition is sound. The two concepts must be explained *together*: neither can be taken as given in advance of the other, so that the other can be explained in terms of it. The concept of truth has its home within a theory of meaning, within which it is an essential theoretical notion. It cannot be explained by stipulating that the principles of semantic shift are to hold universally, useful as those principles may often be in accounting for uses of the term "true" made in day-to-day discourse. Those principles are to be judged as holding or not holding in the light of our conception of truth; and our conception of truth is responsible to the theory of meaning in accordance with which our language is to be understood.

3

STATEMENTS ABOUT THE PAST

Our problem is to fashion a theory of meaning that yields an account of use. The most obvious way in which to do this is to adopt a theory whose central notion is itself a feature of use, and this means either a justificationist theory or a pragmatist one. Since, as I have argued, nothing hangs upon the choice between them, because they will come to the same in the end, I shall concentrate upon the justificationist theory. What is the conception of truth appropriate to a justificationist theory of meaning? Plainly, it must turn on the notion of our being justified in asserting a statement. It is evident at the outset that the word "our" must be taken in a collective, not a distributive, sense. In learning language, we learn not only when it is right to say certain things and what responses certain utterances evoke, but how to respond to the utterances of others; such responses include acting on the truth of what others assert. A child who had learned only when he was right to come out with simple assertoric utterances, such as "Doggie" when a dog was in sight, would serve as an extension of adults' range of observation, but could not yet be credited with saying that anything was so: he can be credited with that only when he has learned to treat the utterances of others as extending *his* range of observation. It is intrinsic to the use of language that we accept the testimony of others: to believe what we are told is the default response. Language binds us into society.

The intuitionist theory of meaning applies only to mathematical statements, whereas a justificationist theory is intended to apply to the language as a whole. The fundamental difference between the two lies in the fact that, whereas a means of deciding a range of mathematical statements or any other effective mathematical procedure, if available at all, is permanently available, the opportunity to decide whether or not an empirical statement holds good may be lost: what can be effectively decided now will no longer be effectively decidable next year, nor, perhaps, next week.

We can gain some insight into the matter from the intuitionistic theory of meaning, all the same. Intuitionistic semantics specifies the meaning of each logical constant by laying down what is to count as a proof of a statement of which it is the principal operator. But only a little reflection is needed to show that "proof" in this context means something narrower than an intuitively valid deductive argument. A proof of a statement of the form "A → B" is specified to be an operation that can be recognized as taking any proof of A into a proof of B. An argument employing *modus ponens* is, in that respect, intuitively valid by anyone's standards: so, if what was here meant by "proof" was anything that would count as an intuitively valid argument, anything whatever would serve, according to the specification of the meaning of the connective →, as a proof of "A → B," since by *modus ponens* we could take it and any proof of A into a proof of B. The same applies to the rule of universal instantiation. A proof of a universally quantified statement "$\forall x \, A(x)$" is specified to be an operation that can be recognized as taking any element of the domain into a proof of the corresponding instance: plainly the proof of the instance cannot be allowed to appeal to universal instantiation, on pain of trivializing the specification of the meaning of $\forall$. Clearly, by "proof" in these contexts must be meant an especially direct kind of proof, which may naturally be called a canonical proof.

Plainly, however, if a canonical proof were to be demanded of anyone who purported to have proved a statement, it would be impossible for him to appeal to theorems previously proved. If a previous theorem was a universal statement, he would be unable to appeal to it to justify invoking an instance of it in the course of his proof: he would have actually to apply the operation embodied in the proof of the earlier theorem to obtain a canonical proof of that instance. This would not only greatly increase the length of his proof, perhaps beyond manageability; it would also stultify the entire practice of storing up mathematical information. As Frege remarked, theorems and their proofs store up deductive routines which do not have to be gone over again, but can simply be appealed to. That is why elimination rules such as *modus ponens* and universal instantiation that cannot appear in the body of a canonical proof can be employed in an intuitively valid demonstration.

The property that we seek to preserve in an intuitively valid argument, which is also the property required to justify asserting a mathematical statement, is therefore not possession of a canonical proof: it is having an effective means—a means effective in principle, even if too laborious for practice—of constructing a canonical proof. In mathematics, a constructive proof is one that shows how to prove the conclusion, given that we can prove the premises. Thus Euler's solution of the Königberg bridge problem shows how to find, from an itinerary involving the crossing of every bridge, a bridge it involved crossing twice. In an empirical case in which a walker has been observed to cross every bridge, we may infer that he has crossed some bridge two or more times. But it does not follow that, if we have verified the premise, we can verify the conclusion. We can easily conceive of observers stationed at each bridge, each of whom leaves his post as soon as he sees the walker crossing that bridge but reports only later without giving the time of crossing; we have then no means of identifying a bridge he has crossed twice. In the empirical case, therefore, the conclusion of a valid argument from premises that have been verified is guaranteed to be such that it *could have been* verified, not that we can any longer verify it. If a mathematical statement could have been verified, then it can still be verified, but that is not so for an empirical statement. We ought not to demand a stricter standard for valid deductive arguments about empirical matters than we do for those about mathematical matters. The difference between the two cases requires us to place a lighter burden on the conclusion for it to be true and hence to be believed.

This conclusion—this conception of the notion of truth appropriate to a justificationist account of meaning—must come as a relief to anyone attracted to such an account of meaning yet troubled about the reality of the past. If that account of meaning demanded that we allow as true only those statements about the past supported by present memories and present evidence, then large tracts of the past would continually vanish as all traces of them dissipate. We should be committed to a metaphysical conception according to which nothing exists but the present: the past would be a mere construct out of whatever in the present we treat as being traces of it. We could not so much as think of a statement about the past as having once been true, though now devoid of truth-value, save in terms of present evidence that evidence for its truth once existed. This conception, though not incoherent, is repugnant: we cannot lightly shake off the conviction that what makes a statement about the past true, if it is true, is independent of whether there is *now* any ground that we have or could discover for asserting it. But if the truth of a proposition consists of its being the case that someone suitably placed *could have* verified it, or have found a cogent ground for asserting it, then our conviction is vindicated. On this conception of truth, a statement about the past could be true if someone at the relevant time could have verified it, even though all reason for asserting it may have blown away.

For convenience, I shall use the term "verify" to cover what falls short of verifying a statement in the strict sense; I shall treat it as covering also possession of grounds sufficiently compelling to warrant asserting the statement. Such grounds would *justify* the assertion, which is why I am speaking of a "justificationist" rather than a "verificationist" account of meaning. It is of interest to seek to make this notion precise; but that is not what concerns us in the immediate context.

I confess to being in just the position of the thinker inclined to a justificationist theory of meaning but troubled about the reality of the past. I am indeed attracted by a justificationist account of meaning; at the same time, I have long been worried about reconciling the reality of the past with that account. Many years ago, I wrote and published an article to explore the issue.[9] When I began to write it, I had hoped to arrive at one or the other conclusion: that antirealism about the past was a benign and acceptable view; or that it was incoherent, and that its incoherence would expose a fallacy in the argument for a justificationist theory of meaning. In the result, the conclusion that I reached was the most disappointing possible. Antirealism about the past was *not* incoherent; but it was not believable, either. I have been perplexed by this matter ever since.

It is not enough to adopt the formula "what could have been verified" as encapsulating a satisfactory justificationist conception of truth. We have not vindicated such a conception. We have not shown how, if meaning is to be explained in accordance with a justificationist theory, a speaker may be supposed to acquire a tacit grasp of the notion of truth so conceived. We have merely argued that, if a justificationist is to allow the validity of constructive deductive arguments—those that provide a means of verifying the conclusion, given a sufficiently detailed verification of the premises—he must admit the capacity of a statement to have been verified as a sufficient condition of its truth. The verification of the premises may not have been sufficiently detailed. Even though the argument may convince us that it must have been possible to verify the conclusion, the time for doing so may have passed. If that conclusion relates to the distant, or often even to the fairly recent, past, it will almost certainly have done so. When a constructively valid argument relates to the past, it is possible that we should have a record of its premises having been quite conclusively verified, but that a verification of its conclusion is now forever beyond our reach. But all this shows is that an adherent of a justificationist theory of meaning must choose either of two positions: (1) to deny that constructive arguments, when applied to empirical situations, and particularly to those that lie in the past, are always valid; and (2) to admit that the mere possibility of its having been verified—in an appropriate sense of "possibility"—is a sufficient condition for the truth of a statement. It does *not* establish that truth is to be *identified* with the possibility of being or having been verified; it does not show that that is the conception of truth at which a speaker will arrive if a justificationist theory of meaning is correct.

The justificationist therefore needs to engage in a good deal more argument before he is entitled to claim that the dilemma about the reality of the past has been resolved. Above all, he needs to supply a plausible account of our understanding of statements about the past, and of how we come by that understanding, for it was an application to such statements of the general form of justificationist—or antirealist—considerations about the acquisition of understanding that drove him in the first place to regard an understanding of the past tense as consisting in a grasp of what would *now* warrant or justify assertions concerning the past.

How do we come by an understanding of statements about

what is spatially remote? A child first learns to grasp the three-dimensional disposition of the contents of a small space, such as a room in a house or a small garden. He then learns the layout of some adjacent such spaces—first the rooms in a house, and next the neighboring houses to his own. He then progresses to the construction of a mental map of his near surroundings—the streets and parks or the fields and woods to which he can walk. He is learning the conception of things—houses, trees, pools, rivers—as being disposed in three-dimensional space, and of movable things—animals, people, cars, clouds, birds, airplanes—as moving about in that space. At each of these stages, it is given to him to connect the concept of a place with that of his own movement, that is, of his going to that place. He comes to grasp the notion of distance, and to understand the relation of the distance between two things to the time that it takes to get from one to the other; the conceptual connection between space and time is very fundamental indeed. This connection is not completely tight: there are places he can observe but cannot go to, such as the air in which birds and kites fly, the sky in which the clouds move: but—although he may need to be corrected about rainbows—it is crucial that he understands the birds and clouds as objects of which it can be asked how far away they are, and that are hence in the same space as we are. Obviously, the spatial range of which he grows aware progressively expands: he is taken by car or train to distant places, and later taught first the use of a map and then that of a globe. To understand a globe, he has of course to form a conception of the Earth as a whole and as roughly spherical in shape and having an interior. As the range of places of which the child can conceive grows greater, he retains his primal understanding that it makes sense to ask, of any place, what is happening there now. At a late stage, he comes to understand that the heavenly bodies, the moon, the sun, and the stars, are material bodies too, located at great distances which are still expressible in terms of the miles by which we measure terrestrial ones. He may or may not eventually acquire a grasp of special relativity, which will require a thoroughgoing revision of the concepts of space and of time as he has acquired these in the gradual course of forming ever more extended a conception. Possibly we may find a way of educating adolescents so that no such conceptual revolution is required; at present we are not able to do that.

What is important for us in this process of coming to understand reference to places more or less distant from that which we occupy is that it requires the mental construction of a grid—a system of coordinates by reference to which different places can be specified; for coming to understand reference to different times likewise requires the mental construction of a grid, though in this case only a linear one. The process of learning to comprehend reference to different places at first sight wars only to a minor extent with a simple justificationist account of understanding. At an early stage of a child's intellectual growth, it is natural for him to interpret statements about how things are at some other place in terms of going to that place and making the required observations; one may not want to do this, but the possibility of doing so gives the content of statements of this kind. The interpretation will not do when it is impossible to reach the place in question sufficiently quickly to make the necessary observations. We have then to conceive of going to that place and determining whether the statement held good there at the time at which it was made. This of course raises the problem of our understanding of statements about the past, so there is nothing special about statements about remote places that causes embarrassment to the justificationist.

A child begins to learn the use of the future tense from expressions of intention, in particular both threats and promises, made by his parents or other adults: he comes to understand the succession of days, and so to form a grid that stretches forward. At the same time, he starts to learn the use of the past tense, and so to extend the grid backward. He is given the past tense when he comes out with avowals of his own memories, and when adults evoke his memories by recalling events in their recent joint past. Realist accounts of thought and linguistic understanding routinely invoke the conception of knowing what it is for such-and-such a state of affairs to obtain or for such-and-such a type of event to take place. This becomes problematic when the state of affairs or type of event is one that cannot be directly recognized as obtaining or taking place; but this is not a problem to do with the past tense as such, and we may assume without loss of generality that the statements made to the child about the past, or those of his utterances that are interpreted as tantamount to such statements, all concern states of affairs or types of event that can be directly recognized when they presently take place or have just taken place. With this reservation, we have no difficulty with the notion of knowing what it is for such-and-such a state of affairs to obtain or for such-and-such a type of event to take place: to know this is to be able to recognize the state of affairs as obtaining or the event as occurring when suitably placed to observe it. Nor is there as yet anything problematic about the conception the child acquires of what renders true a statement about the future or one about the past. To establish the truth of a statement about the future, it is necessary to wait for the required length of time, and then to observe whether the state of affairs or event foretold obtains or occurs. To establish the truth of a statement about the past, one must rely on one's own memory or that of others.

So far, then, it appears that the child's understanding is perfectly in accord with a justificationist account of meaning. His understanding of statements about the past must indeed be enlarged so as to connect them not only with memories but also with traces of past occurrences: he must learn to say things like, "He has left the book on the piano," "She must have switched the heat on when she went downstairs," "The cat seems to have killed a bird on the lawn," and the like; but of course this enlargement remains fully consonant with the justificationist account of the meaning of statements about the past. But caution is required in acknowledging this harmony between a child's understanding at an early stage of his conceptual development and the account of understanding derived from a justificationist account of meaning.

A gap already begins to appear between what establishes a statement as true and what it says holds good. Nothing analogous can be found in the intuitionistic account of the understanding of a mathematical statement. You understand such a statement, according to the intuitionists, if you are able to recognize a proof of it when presented with it. It can be established as true by obtaining such a proof; and what it says is that there is such a proof. The proof is simultaneously what is required to establish the statement as true and that of which an assertion of it warrants the existence. This is equally so for many empirical statements. For instance, the canonical way of establishing the truth of such a statement as "There are seventeen apricots in that bowl" is to count the apricots and find that they come to seventeen. And this is just what the statement says, namely that, if you count the apricots, you will find that they come to seventeen. There is no gap here.

The gap between what verifies a statement and what that statement says becomes apparent with empirical statements about how things are in another place. The most direct way available to us of verifying such a statement is to go to that place and observe that that is how things are there, and a grasp of this is integral to the child's coming to understand the meaning of such a statement. But that that is what you would observe if you went there is not what the statement *says*; a child who thought that would not yet have come even to the fundamental stage of understanding statements about other places. We noted that it is integral to the process of learning language not only that an infant learns to give voice to what he himself has observed (as well as to his wants), but also that he learns to grasp the utterances of others as informing him about the world (as well as telling him what he is to do). In the process, he has to make the different pieces of information he receives, from his own observation and from what others tell him, consistent with one another, which will often require that he modify them: they have to cohere into a single intelligible picture of the world. The formation of the mental spatiotemporal grid that his understanding of statements about other places and about past and future times requires him to construct involves that he comprehends such statements as locating states of affairs and events at points on that spatiotemporal grid. His grasp of what states of affairs and types of event those are derives from the ability he has acquired to recognize them when he observes them. When they are said to obtain or to have occurred elsewhere, he knows that he would have to go to that place in order to observe them, and thus to establish the truth of what is said. But that is not what he takes what he is told as *saying*. What it says is that at that particular location on the spatial map is something of a kind he can recognize when he himself is at the right location.

The distinction just drawn between what is needed to establish a statement as true and what the statement says needs careful scrutiny. If we adopt it, we take a very decided lurch in the direction of a truth-conditional account of meaning, and thus of a realist account of our thought and language. In drawing the distinction, I have deliberately avoided invoking the notion of meaning. There is a strong temptation to say such things as "The statement 'A rowing race is taking place at place *q*' does not *mean* that, if you were to go to *q*, you would observe a rowing race" and "The statement 'It rained here yesterday' does not *mean* that those who were here yesterday remember its raining": but appeal to the notion of meaning in making the point begs the question. The justificationist theory of meaning takes the meaning of a form of statement to be given by what is needed to establish it as true. A radical justificationist regards this as being that in virtue of which the statement is true, if it *is* true. That is why the antirealist about the past, in my paper of long ago on "The Reality of the Past," ended by holding that there only ever *is* what exists in the present, and hence that a statement about the past, if true at all, can be true only in virtue of what *now* exists or holds good. He cannot allow that such a statement can now be established, if at all, only by what lies in the present, but that it is not itself *about* the present, and that what it says is not anything about the present. We normally suppose that a statement about the past, if true, is rendered true by what lies in the past: hence, although in one sense the past is no more, it must in a definite sense still possess a shadowy existence, since otherwise there would be nothing to render statements about the past true or false. But if someone is genuinely an antirealist about the past, he thinks that the past, as the past, retains no existence whatever: the past survives only in its present traces, including memories. That is why, in distinguishing between what can establish a statement about the past as true and what it is that that statement says, we are repudiating antirealism about the past.

The antirealist's idea that the past is genuinely no more and does not possess even the shadowy existence needed for it to render statements about it true or false has a certain attraction, even though it conflicts with our natural realism about the past. But the idea that other places do not of themselves exist, but subsist only in their effects on where we are now, has no attraction whatever; this is why I discussed the child's learning to understand statements about other places before talking about his learning to understand statements about other times. At least as far as places on or near the Earth's surface are concerned—or in virtue of space travel, we should perhaps say within the inner solar system—to adopt such an idea would make us solipsists: it would run counter to the principle that we each must accept as true what any of us has established as true, that verification is not an individual but a collective activity.

As already remarked, according to the justificationist theory of meaning, the meaning of a form of statement is constituted by what is needed to establish it as true. So does the gap that there may be between what is needed to establish a statement as true and what the statement says demand that we add a further component to its account of meaning: to allow that, as well as what is needed to establish a statement as true, there is also what the statement is understood as saying? Well, *why* do we attribute to the child an awareness that what the statement "Your sister must now be sitting down to her breakfast" says is not that, if he were to go to where his sister is, he would observe her having her breakfast, even though he knows that that would be the surest way of making sure that the statement was true? We do so because we credit the child with a consciousness that this would not be the most *direct* way of verifying the statement. Just as with mathematical statements, understood intuitionistically, so we need a distinction between the canonical, or most direct, way of establishing a statement as true and the legitimate, but indirect, means of doing so. The canonical way of doing so will always be that which corresponds to the composition of the statement and the way the meanings of the words that make it up are given. Thus a casual glance may be all that is needed to confirm the statement "It is either raining or hailing," but this is not yet the canonical means of doing so: in virtue of the meaning of the connective "or," the canonical way to do so must be to establish either that it is raining or that it is hailing. Consider the statement, already used as an example, "There are 17 apricots in that bowl." Virtually anyone, asked to characterize the meaning of that statement, and certainly anyone disposed to explain the meaning of a statement in terms of how we find out that it is true, would talk in this connection about counting: counting the apricots is the direct or canonical method of establishing its truth. But suppose I have only just put the apricots in the bowl, having just bought them and having bought nothing else. Then, if I find I have spent $2.89, I can conclude that there are 17 apricots in the bowl, since 289 is the square of 17 and I know that they did not cost $2.89 each, and I know that they cost more than 1 cent apiece. This is a perfectly cogent piece of reasoning, but it is not a direct or canonical way of establishing the truth of my conclusion.

We attribute to the child a grasp, doubtless inchoate, of the difference between a direct and an indirect way of making sure that something is so. Why should we credit him with regarding the procedure of taking a journey to a place and observing what is there as no more than an indirect way of establishing the truth of a statement about how things are there? Well, what is the alternative? Let us grant to the child an ability to tell where he is—by no means in all cases an easy thing to do, as the child will know if he has ever lost his way. But we shall not attribute to him an understanding of what, in general, it means to say that an event of a certain kind is happening at such-and-such a place if all he knows is how to determine when he is in that place and how to observe whether an event of that kind is happening there. He must indeed know that if he is to be credited with an understanding of statements of that type. But he must also understand that already to be in the place referred to, and to observe what is taking place there, is the only *direct* way to verify the statement; that it may be true even though such a direct verification of it is not available; and that its truth is capable of being indirectly established. In other words, he must have advanced well beyond the point of grasping only statements of the most elementary kind, those that we are able to verify by immediate observations and that are falsified by our failing to make such observations. "It is now raining (here)" is such an elementary statement. To verify it, you need only look about you or hold out your hand, or, if you are indoors, look out of the window or front door: if you do not then see or feel that it is raining, you know that it is *not* raining. There is seldom any role for the indirect verification of such elementary statements to play.

But, although a statement that a certain event is occurring in a certain place can be directly verified by the child's establishing that he is in that place and observing the occurrence of that event, it is not falsified by his establishing that he is *not* in that place. The statement does not mean that he is in that place and can observe the occurrence of the event: rather, it has the conditional meaning that, if he were in that place, he would be able to observe the event's occurrence. It therefore follows that any evidence the child may have for the truth of the statement—including his traveling to that place and observing the occurrence of that event—must be categorized as indirect.

This might be objected to, on the ground that the child's understanding of reference to different places is founded upon his grasp of how it is possible—when it *is* possible—to get to them. His grasp of the meaning of a statement about what is happening at a distant place therefore incorporates the conception of getting to that place and observing how things are there. To some extent this is correct. Even an adult may have no better grasp of where some street in his town, or some nearby town, is located than a knowledge of a route to it. But this is only a partial grasp of where that street or town is. For one whose entire understanding of the meanings of expressions referring to that street or town was constituted by a knowledge of a route to it, it would be unintelligible to speak of a different or better route to that street or town: reached by a different route, it could not be for him the *same* street or town. That is why a full understanding of references to different places, and hence of statements about what is happening elsewhere, demands the conception—however rudimentary—of a spatial grid upon which a map may be constructed.

Thus reflection upon our understanding of statements about what states of affairs obtain, or what events are occurring, in other places forces the justificationist a certain distance in the direction of realism.

4

THE SEMANTICS
OF THE PAST TENSE

At the end of the last chapter it was acknowledged
that reflection upon our understanding of statements about what states of affairs obtain, or what
events are occurring, in other places forces the justificationist a certain distance in the direction of realism. The grasp of such a statement falls into two
parts: one is an understanding of what it is for a state
of affairs of the type in question to obtain or an
event of the type in question to occur; the other is
our knowledge of how to locate it on the grid which
serves to particularize the place referred to. This
bears a resemblance to the realist's idea that our
understanding of a statement ascribing some property to an object is constituted by a knowledge of
what it is for an arbitrary object to have that property, together with an understanding of reference to
that object. The justificationist may still explain the
former constituent—our grasp of the relevant type
of state of affairs or of event—in terms of our
learned ability to recognize that state of affairs as
obtaining, or that event as taking place, here and
now. But he must relinquish any idea he had that our
understanding of statements of this kind has only

one ingredient, rather than two: that is, that it is constituted by a knowledge of what affords a ground for accepting each such statement as a whole. It indeed remains, for him, integral to that understanding that we are able to recognize evidence for accepting it, and moreover, that we know that the most nearly direct grounds for doing so are supplied by going to the place in question and observing how things are, or what is going on, there. But it is also essential to a sound account of our understanding of such statements that any evidence to be gathered by those who are not now in the place referred to must count as indirect.

The child's conception of the spatial grid will of course undergo refinement as he matures. He will first acquire the knowledge that the Earth approximates to a sphere in shape; then he will learn the rudiments of astronomy. Despite the boastfulness of contemporary scientists, it took the human race a long time to grasp the rudiments of astronomy. If civilization lasts that long, which I seriously doubt, I should be surprised to be told that five centuries from now people would not regard the conceptions of present-day cosmologists as being as far from the truth as we regard the Ptolemaic system.

It is of course evident that many states of affairs and many occurrences cannot be recognized as obtaining or taking place by mere observation. The foregoing discussion of statements about other places was in effect confined to those which describe states of affairs and events which can be so recognized as obtaining or as happening in some other place. This was simply to isolate the matter of our understanding of reference to other places: in order to isolate it, we must assume it as already known what it is to conceive of the state of affairs or event in question as obtaining or taking place, and the most straightforward way to do this is to assume that it is one that can be recognized by simple observation.

Realists may well react to the whole discussion of how we acquire an understanding of statements about other places as banal.

Realists think of our understanding of all statements whatever as consisting in the knowledge of what it is for them to be true. Most realists simply help themselves to this notion: they show little interest in explaining what our conception of what it is for statements of different kinds to be true consists of, let alone how we come by such conceptions. The foregoing exploration of a child's coming to understand statements about other places had a dual purpose. One motive was to show that a justificationist is forced, if he aspires to give a credible explanation of our understanding of our language, to represent the senses of such statements as bipartite rather than homogeneous. The other was to illustrate how he may concede this without abandoning the general principle of justificationism. He is not driven by the need to make this concession to surrender utterly to realism: he can still broadly maintain the conception of meaning with which he started.

The notion of the truth of a mathematical statement appropriate to a constructivist interpretation of its meaning is that it consists of our possession of a means, effective in principle—that is, prescinding from the limitations of our practical abilities and of the time at our disposal—of constructing a canonical proof of it. There is room here for dispute over whether it is necessary that we should *know* that these means will yield a canonical proof of that very statement, or whether it is sufficient that, if applied, they would in fact yield a proof of that statement. It seems preferable to adopt the laxer view. It is accepted that we are entitled to assert a disjunctive statement if we possess a method, effective in principle, of finding a proof of one or other disjunct. We do not need to know of which of the two disjuncts this method would, if applied, yield a proof, only that it would yield a proof of one or the other. Likewise, we are entitled to assert an existential statement if we possess a method, effective in principle, of finding a proof of some instance of it: for instance, to assert a statement "$\exists x\, A(x)$," where the variable ranges over the natural numbers, if we possess an effective method of finding a proof of some specific statement "A(n)." The connection, argued for in chapter 2, between the assertoric content of a statement and its truth implies that, in the first case, if we possess a method of the given kind, then the disjunctive statement is true, and that, in the second case, if we possess a method of the kind in question, then the existential statement is true. It is not in itself wholly abhorrent to allow that a disjunctive statement may be true even though neither of its disjuncts is true: without appealing to quantum logic, we have only to consider vague statements: the statement "That feature is either a hill or a mountain" may well be definitely true even though neither "That feature is a hill" nor "That feature is a mountain" is definitely true. We are more reluctant to allow that, even in the presence of vagueness, an existential statement may be true even though none of its instances is true. But if we deny the truth of "There is a number for which that number of grains of sand fails to make a heap, but the addition of one more grain of sand will make a heap," we shall fall into the Sorites paradox; but there is surely no number n such that "n grains of sand do not make a heap, although $n + 1$ grains of sand do" is true.

If we set aside the anomalies arising from vagueness, we may say that, for any disjunctive statement which we are entitled to assert, one or the other of the disjuncts must be true, even if we do not know which, and that, for any existential statement which we are entitled to assert, one or the other of its instances must be true, even if we do not know which. That disjunct or that instance would be true in virtue of our possessing a procedure that *would* in fact, if applied, yield a proof of it: we need not know that it would do so. So the condition for the truth of a mathematical statement, under this conception, would be a hypothetical one. It is that we are in possession of an effective procedure such that, if we were to apply it, we should obtain—should in fact obtain—a proof of that statement. On any constructivist view, however, as we ordinarily understand constructivism, the replacement of what we *know* by what *is so*—what in fact holds good—applies only to the outcome of the procedure. It is not enough that there should in fact *be* such a procedure: we have to *know* of that procedure, and know that it will terminate with a proof of a statement in the right class (one of the disjuncts or one of the instances), even though we do not need to know that it will yield a proof of the very statement that is true in virtue of it.

What, then, should a justificationist require for a statement about what is happening at a given place to be true? In speaking of a child's acquiring an understanding of statements referring to particular places, we were concerned with his coming to understand statements about *other* places, i.e., places other than where he was. But we must not speak in this way in general: we are not considering the question in the light of a solipsistic theory of meaning. We are entitled to accept what others tell us on the basis of their observations. That is how we use our language; by means of it we distribute information among ourselves, as well as from past observers to later generations. So there is direct evidence for the truth of a statement that something is occurring at a certain place provided that someone is observing it there.

Our discussion has been quite casual about the notion of observation: ought it to be confined to observation by the unaided senses, or ought it to comprise also observation by means of instruments? For myself, I am inclined to say that, when we are concerned to specify the most *direct* means of establishing that an event of a certain type occurred, the use of instruments should count as observation only when such an event cannot be observed without them; but the point is not germane to our present inquiry. What is meant by "someone" is another important question: must this be a human being? It is plausible that it should cover any creature with whom we might be able to communicate—dolphins, perhaps, eventually; but again the point is not immediately relevant. Furthermore, a more sophisticated account than that just sketched would not require an observer to be at the very place in question, but only to be sufficiently close to it to observe an event of the given kind, which, if we are allowing observation by means of instruments, need not, for some events, be very close at all. Likewise, when we are considering events taking place at an astronomical distance from any observer, we should not be concerned with those occurring at the time the observation is made, but with ones occurring previously to it by the time taken by a light-signal to reach him. But these, and many others, are refinements needed for an adequate systematic account; they are not relevant to the questions that have been concerning us.

What *is* relevant is the criterion for the truth of statements about what is happening in a place in which there is no observer, or to which there is none sufficiently close. The natural suggestion is that the criterion is expressible by a conditional: that if someone were to have been in or sufficiently close to that place at the relevant time, he would have observed an event of that kind. This is certainly enough to vindicate indirect ways of finding out what is happening in places beyond the scope of any observer; but it is not enough to vindicate the principle of bivalence for such statements. If we have an effective method of deciding some mathematical statement A—say the statement that some large number is prime—then we are entitled to assert "$A \lor \neg A$"; and from what was said earlier it follows that A must be considered either true or false. It is true if our decision method, if it had been applied, would have yielded an affirmative result, false if it would have yielded a negative result. Now we certainly are not in general entitled to assume that every conditional with an unfulfilled antecedent either determinately holds good or determinately fails: the most resolute realist would not make such an assumption, because the consequent might depend upon some factor not mentioned in the antecedent. But the assumption *is* plausible for a conditional of the form, "If the decision method were applied, it would yield an affirmative result." It is plausible because the outcome of the decision procedure is unaffected, at each step, by external factors, but is internally determined. That is not so with the empirical procedure of moving to a place and observing what is taking place there: the outcome of this procedure *is* determined by factors external to it. To assume that there is a definite truth about what would be observed if there were an observer at a place where in fact there is not is to assume that the world is determinate independently of our experience; and this is a realist assumption, not readily defended from justificationist premises.

A justificationist semantics allows for there being gaps in reality: questions for which there is no answer containing any truth of the matter one way or another. To say that God must know the answer to any such question begs the question. If there is a truth of the matter, then God must know it; but if there is no truth of the matter, there is nothing for God to know. Gaps in reality are like gaps in a fictional world. If, when asked whether Laertes was left-handed or right-handed, Shakespeare would have had no answer to give, then the question *has* no answer: there is no truth of the matter. Naturally, there will be many cases in which we have indirect grounds for saying how things are at some place where there is no observer; but, on justificationist principles, we are not entitled to assume that there must always be some true answer to a question about such a matter.

But does not the admission of such gaps conflict with the principle that the same logical principles must govern statements about places unobserved as govern those about places that are observed? If there is an effective means, by making the required observations, of deciding whether an event of some kind K is taking place here and now, then we may assert that either an event of the kind K is taking place or it is not, whether we trouble ourselves to make the required observations or not. So, in accordance with the principle that the same logical laws must govern all empirical statements, irrespective of their spatiotemporal reference, we must recognize it as legitimate to assert, of any place and time, that either an event of the kind K occurred or will occur in that place at that time or it did or will not. However, the principle of the preservation of logical laws does not extend to the preservation of semantic theses. The law of excluded middle, in cases when it holds good of the here and now, must be preserved as applying to the there and then; but we cannot argue, as we did before, from the validity of excluded middle to the semantic thesis of bivalence. We do not need, and have not the right, to maintain that either the statement that an event of the kind K occurred or will occur at the given place and time is determinately true or is determinately false. It may be uncomfortable to admit that a disjunctive statement may be true although truth attaches to neither of the disjuncts; but it is a discomfort to which we may need to adjust. A statement that an event is occurring in a place devoid of observers is true if such an event could have been observed had an observer been present. An observer at that place, if he had made the required observations, would either have observed the occurrence of an event of kind K or the nonoccurrence of such an event: so the statement that an event of that kind either did or did not occur there is true. But we do not have a basis to argue that either the statement that such an event occurred or the statement that no such event occurred is true. The validity of a particular case of the law of excluded middle is no safeguard against a gap in reality.

Direct evidence for the truth of an empirical statement does not in general consist of bare observations, but may comprise an inferential component. At one end of a scale lie reports of observation, at the other mathematical theorems, established by pure deductive reasoning. Most statements we make lie between these end points: they are to be directly established by reasoning based on observation. These include statements about physical conditions that could not be observed—conditions in the interior of the sun, in a super-nova, within a black hole—and statements about conditions before there were any observers. We form judgments about such matters by reasoning, in accordance with our physical theories, from obser-vations remote from our conclusions. The contrast here is not metaphysical, but merely between what can be established by sim-ple observation and what it requires inference to arrive at.

There is a genuinely metaphysical disagreement about the effect that the past tense has upon the meaning of a sentence. It is not merely consistent with a justificationist theory of meaning to take direct evidence for the truth of a statement about the past to consist of observations made from a suitable distance at the rele-vant past time, but essential so to take it, if the theory is to treat evidence, not as what an individual subject possesses, but as some-thing in principle available to us collectively. We need a theory of meaning for our common language, not for an idiolect. Against this, the antirealist about the past holds that evidence for a state-ment about a past event can consist only in present memories or presently observable traces of the event. This is the metaphysical controversy we are exploring.

Our discussion of statements about other places was, of course, intended as analogue for inquiring into our understanding of state-ments about other times. Here, too, the child must acquire the con-ception of a grid: indeed, he must have not merely a spatial and a temporal grid, but a spatiotemporal grid. But can we attribute to the child a recognition that present evidence for the truth of a state-ment concerning another time is indirect? Must he, to have acquired an understanding of the past and future tenses, grasp that what a statement couched in either of those tenses *says* is not that such evidence exists, but, rather, that that is how things were or will be at the indicated position on the temporal grid? Do we have a true analogy with his understanding of statements about other places?

If the analogy is a true one, then what is *said* by a statement in a tense other than the present is that a certain event took place or will take place (or that a certain state of affairs obtained or will obtain) at the time and place it refers to. Evidence available at a previous time or at a time later than that at which the event could be observed may establish the truth of the statement or render it probable, but it can only be indirect, since its being available is not what the statement *says*: it is not what renders the statement true. Direct evidence for the truth of the statement can consist only in observations made when and where the event is stated to have taken or to take place; more exactly, at whatever time the event could be observed by an observer placed sufficiently close to observe it.

This might be objected to on justificationist grounds. The only way, it could be argued, in which a statement in the future tense, referring to a specific future time, can be definitively established as true is by waiting until the time referred to arrives, and then making the necessary observations. The objector may, on these grounds, repudiate the idea that such a statement is now *already* true or false, according to how things will be at the specified time; it acquires a definite truth-value only at that time, and does not have one before. But statements about the past, the objector says, ought not to be conceived on the analogy of statements about distant places. We can, in some cases, verify a statement about a distant place by going to that place and observing how things are there. But the whole point concerning statements about the past, he says, is that we *cannot* in principle locate ourselves at the times to which they refer: the past, as the past, is inaccessible. That, he argues, is why we must consider the only direct way of establishing the truth of a statement in the past tense—the only way in principle available to us—to be on the basis of its present traces: the memories of those who witnessed how things were at that time, the reports that have come down to us from past observers, the causal consequences of what happened then. The past is not a region we can travel to, the objector declares: it persists only in its present traces. The past has no other existence: the past, *as* the past, is no more. All that exists—that now exists—is the present: only what now exists can render any statement true or false.

This objector has plunged into some tumultuous metaphysical waters: he is the antirealist about the past resisting the revised version of justificationism that has been argued for here. The mistake the objector makes is to draw the analogy between statements about other places and statements about other times incorrectly. Unless there can be closed timelike world lines, the past is indeed inaccessible. But the direct way of establishing the truth of a statement about a distant place is an observation made by an observer in that place. To take it as consisting in a journey to that place, followed by suitable observations, is to appeal to a theory of meaning in terms of an individual's means of verifying the truth of a statement—the means open to an individual or at best to a small group. That is not, and should not be, the form taken by a justificationist theory of meaning. Such a theory of meaning is concerned with how *we*, collectively, can establish a statement as true. If, as we have been assuming for simplicity, it is a statement of a kind that can be established by observation, then that is the direct way of so establishing it. An observer suitably placed may make such observations, and he may then transmit the information that he has so acquired to others. Someone else to whom this information has been passed on will not himself have made the relevant observations. His personal possession of the information is founded upon testimony; but its original source was founded upon observation. That is one of the central functions of language, namely to spread knowledge to the whole community of those who employ the language. For that reason, a theory of meaning for our language—that is, ultimately, for all intertranslatable languages—cannot be based upon an individual's use of the language as a means of expressing the knowledge that he personally has; it must be based upon our common use of language to express and transmit knowledge accessible to us all. We may of course have indirect evidence for the truth of a statement about a place where no observer was present. Such indirect evidence must show that a suitably located observer could have made observations giving direct grounds for the truth of the statement: that is how indirect evidence is related to direct evidence.

In the same way, direct evidence for the truth of a statement about the past, of the kind that could be a report of an observation when made in the present tense, takes the form of an observation made at the time to which it refers (or at a time when that observation was possible). If someone still living did make such an observation, he may of course report it to others on the strength of his memory of doing so. But it is not only the living who may report their past observations. If we have a written record of what was observed by a witness who is now dead, or an account of the observations that has been passed from that witness down a chain of informants, we are in as good a position to know by testimony that the past event was observed as if we were told by a living observer. Dying does not deprive anyone of the status either of an observer or of an informant: the dead remain members of the community—the community I have been referring to as "we"— with whose collective and imperfectly shared knowledge I have been concerned. Admittedly, most of their messages have been obliterated by time; but many of the dead still communicate with us, not in spiritualist séances and only rarely in visions, but through their words that have been preserved, their writings, their works of art, and their scientific and philosophical theories. For all the messages that have been lost, it remains that statements about the past must count as having been directly established, and therefore as true, if someone observed them to be true at the, or an, appropriate past time.

The argument of this book has been that a justificationist must accept this account of how statements about the past are to be understood because it is incontrovertibly how we do understand them: antirealism about the past does not faithfully represent the manner in which we in fact understand the past tense. It must nevertheless be granted that, in acceding to such an account of statements about the past, the justificationist will have substantially modified his doctrine. If we had a language in which every statement that could be framed admitted of an effective means—effective at least in principle—for deciding its truth or falsity, there would be no practical difference between a justificationist and a truth-conditional explanation of meaning. It is largely because we can readily frame statements that are not in this sense decidable that such a difference exists and has a substantial effect both on the logical laws accepted by the adherents of the two types of meaning theory and on their metaphysical conceptions of reality. Now if we assume that statements of the most primitive type are in principle effectively decidable, the question arises what components of sentence formation import undecidability into our language: what makes it possible for us to frame undecidable statements? I once wrote[9] that there are three linguistic devices that have this effect: quantification over infinite totalities, as expressed by such a word as "never"; the subjunctive conditional form; and the past tense. A justificationist who accepted this analysis would then want to oppose a justificationist account of each of these three linguistic operations to a truth-conditional one. The problem of quantification over infinite totalities arises within mathematics, and we know very well what a platonist or truth-conditional conception of it is like; we also know very well what alternative conception a constructivist mathematician will advance. I have no idea what a truth-conditional explanation of the subjunctive conditional would be; I note that many philosophers of a realist inclination assume without argument that a great range of subjunctive conditionals have determinate truth-values, and believe that the question when and on what grounds it may be legitimately assumed that they do deserves far closer scrutiny than it receives. In both these cases I myself would side with the justificationist. But of the third case, the past tense, I have here been arguing that the correct account is not along purely justificationist lines. An account along purely justificationist lines would embody an untenable antirealist conception of the past. The account that has here been offered of our understanding of the past tense is still justificationist in character, but the theory has been revised in a realist direction. Adopting it does not demand of the justificationist that he repudiate his general principles: he will still hold that a statement about the past can be true only in virtue of an actual or possible direct verification of it. But he will take a more realist attitude to whether such a direct verification was or could have been carried out. In doing so, his theory of meaning has been modified so as to approach realism more closely.

There is a need to look very carefully at topics concerning which realism exerts a very strong pull, and justificationism appears implausible or repugnant. The past tense is one such topic. There are surely others. It may prove that our intuitive revulsion against a full-fledged justificationist attitude to such topics is defensible, or it may prove that it is due to prejudice that we have not properly examined. The most pressing question is whether a generally justificationist account of our understanding of our language can still be maintained in the face of the problems these topics raise, or whether the weight of necessary concessions to realism will make rejection of realism as a comprehensive theory untenable. I do not myself think so, but the question demands much hard reflection.

Observation is ordinarily understood as revealing what would have been so even if the observation had not been made. This is a sophisticated thought, which ought not to be attributed to a child who has been taught to say how things are by looking, feeling, or listening. Rather, it is in part by learning these skills that the child forms the conception of an objective environment independent of his will and of its being observed by him or others, a conception that rounds out the infantile expectations of repeatable surroundings and familiar experiences he has had since the earliest stage of life. He learns what to expect to be still the same when he views it afresh, and what to expect to have altered, in accordance with some process that was then under way; he learns to seek an explanation when such expectations are falsified, in terms of something that went on in the interim. It is the standard practice to treat observation as disclosing some state of affairs, rather than as contributing to creating it: that is the practice in which the child learns to engage. Small children do not need to acquire the notion of an objective feature of the world as they observe it; rather, they need to be instructed which features of their experience are subjective. It is therefore a mistake to argue that a conception of reality as existing independently of being observed must be prior to and inform the observational practice that we learn: it is by learning that practice that we acquire such a conception. It is only at a much later stage that, as adults, we extend our childhood distinction between objective and subjective into that between how things are in themselves and how we human beings perceive them, a distinction far from straightforward. It remains that our primitive grasp of what it is for this or that observable state of affairs to obtain rests on our learned ability to recognize it as obtaining when we observe it.

When, as in quantum mechanics, there is a theoretical ground for thinking that observation disturbs what is observed, it becomes problematic whether there is any reality independent of observation; if there is, it cannot be explained in terms of what could be observed. When the ground is a merely practical one, as in observing a deer or bird liable to run or fly away, there is no reason to reject an explanation of a statement about the creature in terms of what might be observed. Observation is difficult in these circumstances, but might well be made so as to inhibit the creature's flight, with a telescope or by means of camouflage. We need not do this ourselves; it is enough that we can conceive of it.

5

THE METAPHYSICS OF TIME

Disagreements about how we understand statements in the past and future tenses reflect, or generate, disagreements about the metaphysics of time. There are four possible metaphysical positions concerning the reality of the past and the future: either both are real, or neither, or one but not the other. These four views are usually expressed as if "present," "past," and "future" were absolute notions; although we know that they are not, I will formulate them in this manner. The four metaphysical models are, then, as follows.

Model (1) *Only the present is real*. All that constitutes reality is how things are *now*. The past *was* part of reality, but it exists no more. The future *will be* part of reality, but it has not yet come into existence. We may of course generalize this: all that reality consists of at any one time is how things are at that time. Reality—what there is—continually changes: it consists of what there *is*.

At first glance, this model simply embodies what is obvious from our experience of the world. Reality just *does* continually change. The present forms the substance of the world; the past consists of what *has been* present, the future of what *will be* present. Hence all that now exists is what is *now* present.

A moment's further reflection shows that this picture of evanescent reality cannot be sustained. There is, to begin with, the difficulty first raised by St. Augustine. The present has no duration: it is a mere boundary between past and future. But a boundary can exist only if that which it bounds exists. Two regions on a plane surface may be separated by a line, straight or curved. But the line could not exist on its own; it exists only in virtue of the regions that it demarcates.

Furthermore, the thesis that only the present is real denies any truth-value to statements about the past or the future; for, if it were correct, there would be nothing in virtue of which a statement of either type could be true or false, whereas a proposition can be true only if there is something in virtue of which it is true. We must attribute some form of reality either to the past, or to the future, or both.

Model (2) *The future is real, but the past is not.* The future is accessible: we have only to wait to discover what it holds, which is what it has always held. The past, by contrast, is inaccessible. On the radical version of this model, which we may call model (2*), the past has therefore vanished utterly. A past-tense statement may have been true at the time to which it refers, but is no longer either true or false.

On model (2) proper, it is acknowledged that the past has left traces, including our own memories. But, on this more moderate version of the model, those traces, which are part of the present, are all that there is of the past: they constitute it. The physicist John Wheeler has stated the matter correctly: "the past has no existence except as it is recorded in the present." The past has no independent reality.

This model, advocated by C. I. Lewis, A. J. Ayer in his early period, and Jan Lukasiewicz, incorporates the antirealism about the past which has concerned us. It does not deny, as model (1) does, that there is anything that can render a statement about the past true; but it insists that whatever renders a statement about the past true must lie in the present. This seemingly conflicts with the truth-value links, which assuredly govern our use of tensed statements. Such a truth-value link requires that if a statement in the present tense, uttered now, of the form "An event of type K is occurring," is true, then the corresponding statement in the past tense, "An event of type K occurred a year ago," uttered a year hence, must perforce also be true. But this appears to show that the thesis of model (2) cannot be generalized. At any time, you may perform some trivial action, say scratching your right ear. By the truth-value link, if in exactly a year's time you were to say, "I scratched my right ear precisely a year ago," what you said would be true. But it may well be that in a year's time you would have forgotten that trivial action, and that every trace of its occurrence would have dissipated. According to model (2), your statement, "I scratched my right ear precisely a year ago," would *not* be true. It thus appears that the proponent of model (2) cannot respect the truth-value links.

The proponent of model (2), whom, to avoid repetition, we may call Luke, has an escape from this accusation, however. He can escape it because his conception of time immerses him even more thoroughly in time than the proponent of model (1). He declares his complete adherence to the truth-value links. He therefore allows that if exactly a year hence you say, "I scratched my right ear precisely a year ago," your statement will be true, just because, when you say now, "I am scratching my right ear," what you say is true. But in a year's time he will deny that that same statement, "I scratched my right ear precisely a year ago," which you make then, is true, because there will then be no ground for asserting it. If evidence is given him that a year before you had said, "I am now scratching my right ear," he may count this as a ground for the truth of the past-tense statement, made then; if he does not, then, in faithfulness to the truth-value links, he will deny that that earlier statement was true when you made it. By itself, this only shows that it will be possible for Luke to remain verbally faithful to the truth-value links if he varies his assessment of the truth-values of the very same statements. We should normally assume, however, that such variable assessment is inconsistent: it could not be correct at both times. Luke, we should think, can be faithful to the truth-value links only because he is unaware of his inconsistency. This is to misunderstand him. He can perfectly well entertain our hypothesis that you are now scratching your right ear, but that, in a year's time, all effects of your doing so will have dissipated; and he will agree that, in the light of present reality, your statement, made in a year's time, will be true. But he will deny that it follows that, if, in a year's time, he judges that that same statement is not true, he will be judging wrongly. For he will then be judging, not in the light of present reality, but in the light of reality as constituted a year from now; and the contents of reality will have altered in that interval. Luke, as a supporter of model (2), must relativize the truth of a statement, not only to the time of utterance but also to the time of evaluation. For him, the reality in terms of which statements, whenever made, are to be assessed as true or false constantly changes: the traces of events are dissipated and leave nothing to render certain statements true or false. Of course, he does not *say* that a statement may have been true when made but has now ceased to have been true: he will say that it never was true. But he can and does say that a statement about what is happening now may be true but may later be correctly judged not to have been true.

On Luke's conception, reality changes continually, and, with it, the past also changes. Such a conception is not self-contradictory, but it goes very strongly against the grain. Luke honors the truth-value links; but, we are disposed to say, he honors them only with his lips. He agrees that it is what happened a year ago that renders what anyone now says about what happened a year ago true or false. But he does not mean what we mean by saying that it is *what happened in the past* that determines the truth or falsity of our statements about the past; for he uses the phrase, "what happened a year ago" to mean "what year-old events there are present traces of," which is what, for him, determines a statement about how things were a year ago as true, false, or devoid of truth-value. We mean to *oppose* "what happened in the past," as being what renders statements about the past true or false, to present traces of what happened: that, we believe, is the metaphysical principle enshrined by the truth-value links. What is happening now will render true a statement made in a year's time about what happened a year before. The antirealist admits this only in the sense that, according to him, the word "true" *now* has. But, we feel disposed to object, the sense of the word "true" does not change with time: as applied to a statement considered as made at any given time, its sense, and, with it, its application, remain constant. The predicate "is true" may be relativized to the time of utterance, but, we believe, needs no further relativization to the time of evaluation.

Model (2) denies the reality of the past; model (3), as we shall see, denies the reality of the future. But there is a disanalogy between them. Proponents of model (3) standardly say that a statement about the future is not *yet* either true or false, but will become one or the other at the time to which it relates. But the radical version (2*) of model (2) is virtually never proposed. A standard proponent of model (2) does not maintain that every statement about the past lacks present truth-value; nor does he say that such a statement may have been true or false at the time to which it relates, but is now no longer either. The advocate of model (3) can allow statements about the future to have varying degrees of probability: it is just that he does not think they can as yet be determinately true or false. The probability of a statement in the future tense is that of its proving to be, or becoming, true at the relevant time; we are accustomed to this from the practice of betting. But the probability of a statement in the past tense can only be the probability of its being now true; if it has no truth-value, it can have no probability. Model (3) is not blatantly inconsistent with our use of the future tense. But the radical version of model (2) deprives our use of the past tense of all meaning.

Independently of metaphysics, we incontrovertibly have a use of future-tense statements under which they are rendered true or false by how things stand in the present. This is exemplified by a notice in the newspaper of the form "The wedding between Mr. X.Y. and Miss N.M. will not now take place," or the statement "They *were* going to be married, but they are not going to any longer." This use of "will" and "going to" may be called the *present future*. There is no present past. That is to say, while the proponent of model (2) regards our ordinary past tense as having the sense of the present past, we do not have a present-past use of the past tense which we should normally contrast with its ordinary use. Moreover, there is a past present future, which may be opposed to the present present future: "was going to, but is not now going to." But the advocate of model (2) does not countenance a past present past or a future present past that may be opposed to the present present past. He would not say, "She then married Edward in 1825, but did not now do so," or, "She now married Edward in 1825, but probably will not have done so next year."

The ground of these differences lies in our understanding of the direction of causality. We can have evidence for a later or for an earlier event; but only a later event can be prevented. The present future expresses present tendencies toward the future; it says what will happen if things go on as they are now doing. If Jonah's threat that Niniveh was going to be destroyed is understood as having been in the present future, it was true when made; that the destruction did not take place was due to the repentance of the Ninivites, unforeseen by Jonah. Sometimes no prevention may be possible; but that grounds for a prediction are in general subject to that qualification explains why we have the present future use of that tense. A past event cannot be prevented. Evidence for its occurrence may be overridden by later, better evidence, but all we ever have concerning the past is *evidence*. There are no present tendencies toward something's having happened.

To say that some event is no longer going to occur is not to say that the future has changed, and would not be to say that even if we had no future tense other than the present future. But to hold that a statement about the past was true, but now is false, would be to say that the past had changed, just because there are no tendencies toward the past. These various features of our common linguistic practice reflect our conception of how time relates to causality, and are hard to reconcile to any version of model (2). They therefore go to substantiate a justificationist acceptance of the reality of the past, in allowing that the evidence that renders a statement about the past true may itself lie in the past.

If we reject model (2), we may turn to its mirror image, model (3).

Model (3) *The past is part of reality, the future is not.* The future has not yet come to be: it does not yet exist. If it existed, we could know it, since, in virtue of how it is going to be, statements about it could be presently true or false. But we cannot in principle know the future. We may entertain propositions about the future, and may, with good reason, assign them higher or lower probabilities. But, however high the probability of some belief of ours about the future, that belief cannot be *knowledge*, because, so long as the belief continues to be *about the future*, the possibility will always remain open that it will be overturned—overturned by things' not happening in accordance with it. By contrast, the past is a constituent of reality. Once something has happened, it has happened, and nothing can change that. If we know that it has happened, that is genuine knowledge: nothing can overturn our knowledge of its having happened. The passage of time is, as C. D. Broad maintained,[1] a continual growth in the sum total of reality. When an interval of time has passed, reality has increased by just that amount; as a moment that was future becomes present, reality acquires a new surface that it did not have before.

Model (3) is far more palatable to most people than model (2). The past has only the truth-value link, as it were, to protect it; the future can look after itself. Even if the future is now indeterminate, so that statements about it lack definite truth-values, it will eventually arrive in a determinate form: and that is all the reality that the future needs to have. That is to say, model (2), which in effect denied the reality of the past, ran counter to how we think we understand statements in the past tense; but model (3) allows an account of statements in the future tense that is completely in accord with the way in which we use them and understand them. We do not need to credit statements about the future, made now, with a determinate truth-value that they already possess: they *will* be rendered true or false when the time comes, and that is enough to give the future tense the sense that we ascribe to it. Matters stand quite differently with regard to the past. It is not enough to concede that a statement about the past was rendered true or false at the time to which it relates: it must retain that truth-value thereafter. If the past did not continue to possess an enduring reality, our statements about it would not all possess the truth-values that they fleetingly had at, and soon after, the time to which they related. In that case, the past tense could not bear the sense that we believe ourselves to have conferred upon it. A statement about the past must *still* be true or false, according to what happened at the time to which it relates and the truth-value it had then. Otherwise the past tense has no substance.

This defense of model (3) is very familiar, and we are inclined to respond to it with robust agreement. But does it really constitute an argument, or is it mere rhetoric? It is certainly often backed by suasions that have a strong intuitive appeal, but on scrutiny prove, as arguments, to be utterly flimsy. Since the scholastic period, it has been thought a problem to reconcile freedom of action with divine foreknowledge, indeed with there being an *actual* future course of events. The past is fixed, it is said, but the future is fluid: there are numerous possible future courses of events, but no one of them is *the actual* future course of events. Were it not so, we could not affect the future, just as we cannot affect the past: it would be senseless for us to ponder what we shall do, since it would *already* hold good that we shall do one thing or another.

This line of thought of course assumes the falsity of determinism; in my opinion, it is in the right in doing so. Determinism is based on the classical conception of physical magnitudes as absolutely definite, being given, in terms of suitable units, by specific real numbers, rational or irrational. This use of the classical continuum of real numbers as a model for physical reality is in my view mistaken: the model does not fit well. We should do better to think of physical magnitudes as given by small intervals in the rational line: they are intrinsically indefinite.

However this may be, the argument for the indefiniteness of the future lacks all cogency. The illusion derives from the idea that the present truth must compel the future action. The efficacy is in the reverse direction: a proposition about what I am going to do is true in virtue of my later action. Christ's prediction that Peter would deny him did not compel Peter to do so: it was true because he did. If I *knew* what I was going to do, and knew that I knew, I could not, indeed, deliberate over whether or not to do it: but I could consider whether or not I should give my will to doing it. Even if I knew that I was going to do a certain thing, and at that time give my will to doing it, I could consider whether or not I should *now* give my will to it. But the mere supposition that there is now a truth of the matter about what I am going to do is no reason for me not to deliberate, if I do not know what that truth is. Suppose I am playing a card game for very high stakes. After the hands have been dealt, I am told that I once played a hand, which I have now forgotten, in which all the players held just the same cards as now, but not told whether I won or lost. This experiment has been tried on many people; almost all play their hands as they did before. Knowing that it is almost certain how I am going to play does not inhibit me from thinking out my strategy.

The same holds good for the claim that we cannot affect the past. If I know what happened in the past, it would indeed be senseless for me to try to prevent it from having happened, and even more to act so as to bring it about that it happened; and we are indeed seldom in this position with respect to what will happen in the future. But if I do *not* know what happened in the past, there is nothing senseless in my doing something to bring it about, or make it more probable, that some particular thing happened, if I think I know of some means of doing so. If someone prays that something should have happened, he is not acting nonsensically: he is not asking God to make something have happened that did not happen, but only that He should have made it happen.

There is a standard argument to show that, since a given past event has either happened or not happened, it must be either redundant or fruitless to do anything to bring it about that it has happened. This is the precise analogue to an argument for fatalism, to show it either redundant or fruitless to do anything to bring it about that something should subsequently happen, an argument that almost everyone would reject as sophistry. The fatalist argument starts from the premise that the event either will or will not happen. We want to reply that it may be that it will happen precisely because of what we do now to bring it about: not knowing whether it will happen or not, we have no reason to refrain from doing what we believe makes it more probable. If we knew of something we could do that would make it more probable that some event previously took place, but did not knew whether it had taken place or not, we should have no reason to refrain from doing that. To retort that the past event has *already* either happened or not happened, whereas the future event has not *yet* happened or failed to happen, is obviously to assume what it was intended to prove.

There is no logical necessity that causation should always run in the earlier-to-later direction; it is simply our experience that it does so. Apart from prayer, we know of no way of making it more probable that some event should have previously occurred. The direction of causality is a pervasive fact about reality; it is not a ground for denying substance to what lies in one temporal direction from the present moment.

We can direct against model (3) an objection strictly analogous to that with which we opposed model (2). For the constancy of truth-value is as much impugned by the thesis that statements about the future acquire a truth-value only at the time to which they relate as by the supposition that statements about the past are deprived of truth-value as soon as evidence of their truth or falsity is dissipated. It is *what is going to happen in the future* that renders our statements about the future true, when they are true. This platitude is embodied in the truth-value links, just as was the corresponding platitude concerning statements about the past. A proponent of model (3) may protest that he does not regard any statement as acquiring a truth-value other than one it had before. He declares that he does not think that *any* statement in the future tense has a determinate truth-value: only those in the present and past tenses have determinate truth-values, he says. But the truth-value links debar him from adopting this defense. If some event—say, your scratching your right ear—is happening now, the truth-value link demands that the statement, made a year ago, that you would be scratching your right ear in exactly a year's time was true: that it was *then* true, not merely that it would be true in a year's time. The proponent of model (3) will be forced to hold that it may be correct, at a given time, to assign a truth-value to a statement in the future tense made previously but relating to that time. That earlier statement lacked a truth-value when it was made; now it has acquired one. Just like the proponent of model (2), the proponent of model (3) has been compelled to regard the truth-values of statements in the future tense as needing to be relativized to the time of evaluation, and not just to the time at which they are made. What provides any space for such a dual relativization? Model (3) is open to objections precisely analogous to those we admitted as fatal to model (2). If our argument against model (2) was valid, virtually the same argument must be valid against model (3).

It may be replied that model (2) envisaged statements about the past as being *deprived* of truth-values they formerly possessed, whereas model (3) envisages statements about the future as *acquiring* truth-values that they formerly lacked, and that this difference invalidates the argument against model (3) while leaving the parallel argument against model (2) intact. Why should it?

This defense exemplifies a mistake frequently made in philosophical discussions about time. A philosopher wishes to demonstrate an asymmetry between past and future, or between the earlier-to-later direction and its opposite: he wishes, for instance, to demonstrate that the dual of a thesis that holds good of the past does not hold good of the future. His argument turns on the use of some temporally asymmetric expression or pair of expressions, that is, ones that can only be explained by reference to a particular temporal direction. Plainly, such an argument begs the question: the asymmetry he sought to demonstrate was built into the vocabulary by means of which his argument for it was framed. In the present case, "is deprived of" and "acquires" form just such a pair of expressions: the only difference between them relates to the temporal order of a statement's possessing and lacking a truth-value. To insist that the difference affects the validity of an argument and of its dual is to assert no more than that the one concerns the future and the other the past: it is not to give any reason why that should be relevant to their validity.

An escape from this difficulty which some have found attractive is to modify model (3) by denying that we have any future tense for which the truth-value links hold—what we may call a genuine future tense, that is a true dual of the past tense. On this view a statement in the future tense is true or false in virtue only of what holds good at the time it is made; the only legitimate use of that tense is as the present future. It is difficult to maintain that we do not also use it as a genuine future tense. In a future-tense conditional, the sense of the antecedent may, as previously remarked, be future, even though in English its tense may be grammatically present; and this sense must be interpreted as that of the genuine future tense. Indeed, even if we take an expression of intention for the future to be true provided that the speaker really has that intention, the proposition that he intends to make true must, on pain of vacuity, be in the genuine future tense, as is the proposition on whose truth a bet is made. Even if there be some subtle way of construing these examples as not really involving the genuine future tense, the proponent of model (3) cannot be content with arguing that we do not in fact employ the genuine future tense in our language: he must maintain that such a tense would be unintelligible; we could not understand what it would be to have such a tense in the language. This, in the face of the fact that many would maintain that we already have it, is a case difficult to sustain.

The standard arguments for model (3) thus fail, and it seems, therefore, that we must reject it. If we do, we shall have no choice but to adopt the fourth model of time. Models (1) to (3), as here characterized, treat "past" and "future" as absolute terms, which we know that they are not. If we were to adopt any of them, we should need to reformulate it in the light of this fact. Model (4) does not, of itself, require such reformulation. Not having thoroughly internalized relativity theory, we are strongly disposed to think of simultaneity as an absolute relation; indeed, I spoke in chapter 3 of a child's grasping that he can ask, "What is happening there now?" as an essential step in his coming to understand statements about other places. Yet, relativity theory aside, there is no compelling rational ground for the absoluteness of simultaneity. Imagine that there were a permanent dense fog separating the Old World from the New, and that no regularity were detectable in the time taken to travel from one to the other: sometimes only a few days would have passed in the other hemisphere after a traveler's last visit there, sometimes many years. It would then be senseless to ask what had been happening in one half of the Earth at the very time that something happened in the other; yet each half would have its own history.

Model (4) *Past and future are both real.* They are simply regions of reality determined, at any given moment, by our temporal perspective, as it is at that moment. Time is one of the dimensions along which reality varies, as it does along any of the three spatial dimensions; our awareness is one of the respects in which it varies. There is no distinction between past and future in reality; there is no *now* in reality. There is indeed a distinction between one temporal direction and the other; the earlier-to-later direction is that of causal efficacy. Hence we assign to the past those events capable of having a causal influence upon events near us, so that we can receive information from them and of them, but have no means of affecting them; and we assign to the future those events that we can affect, but from which we can receive no information. Time is thus not merely one dimension out of four; but what occupies it in each direction is equally real.

Does not this four-dimensional conception commit the error of *spatializing* time? John McTaggart argued that to deny that being past, present, or future is an objective feature of reality is to delete what is essential to time—change.[2] He himself wished to deny that they were objective features; but he thought he could conclude from this to the unreality of time. On the four-dimensional conception, there is no real change: there is only "Cambridge change," the analogue of saying, "The landscape changes as you travel east." The landscape does not change: it is simply different here and east of here.

The failure of the four-dimensional conception, as so far presented, to take proper account of change is shown by the circularity of its perspectival explanation of "past" and "future." These, on this model, are regions of reality determined, at any given moment, by our temporal perspective, as it is at that moment. Our spatial perspective varies according to where we are at any time; to say that our temporal perspective varies according to when we are at any time would be a misbegotten analogue of this. It varies both according to where we are at that time and according to how things are at that time. The four-dimensional model, as thus described, deprives the world we observe of genuine change; there is only that of our awareness as we travel into the future. The model is grounded on the conception of our consciousness as moving through the static four-dimensional reality along the temporal dimension.

A proponent of the four-dimensional model may deny this. We are, he says, irregular four-dimensional tubes (or hypertubes), with the peculiarity that consciousness attaches only to our temporal cross-sections. Nothing changes: it is just that our different temporal cross-sections are aware of different things. This image is misconceived. Consider a description of other hypertubes, whose axes lie along a spatial dimension. To us these would appear long, very short-lived objects; if we learned that a different consciousness attached to each segment of one of the tubes, we should regard them as strings of distinct creatures. But if we were told that a different consciousness attached to each cross-section of such a tube at an angle orthogonal to its axis, and that the different consciousnesses varied continuously, we could make nothing of this at all. The description of ourselves as hypertubes only makes a kind of sense when interpreted as 4D-speak for a single consciousness moving along the time dimension. The four-dimensional interpretation of model (4) is not tenable after all. It is only an illusion that the version of it that denies all change whatever is intelligible. The version that restricts change to the movement of our consciousness along the temporal dimension is capricious. If it is conceded that there is change, there is no ground for such a restriction. We live in a changing world. Objects—galaxies, stars, planets, plants, and animals—change as they develop and move through space. When the object is a sentient creature, its experiences and observations of its surroundings change; when it is a rational creature, its thoughts and beliefs, its conception of its surroundings, change also. Allowing the reality of both past and future, in the sense that statements in the past and future tenses can have determinate truth-values, not based upon how things are in the present, does not commit us to denying the reality of change and replacing enduring, changing three-dimensional objects with static four-dimensional ones.

What picture, then, should we have of the universe as a whole, as it is in itself rather than from any point of view within it? The question is nonsensical; there is no such thing as a picture from no point of view. Physical reality consists of objects in the world, the changes they undergo and the paths they trace in space-time.

On first appearance, model (4), when divested of its four-dimensional interpretation, is fully consonant with the justificationist understanding of statements about past and future that has been argued for in this book. On such an understanding, direct evidence for a statement that an observable event took place or will take place at any specific past or future date must consist of an observation made at the time to which it relates (or when such an observation is possible); such a statement is true if such an observation was or could have been, or will be or could be, made. The analogy between past and future tenses is complete.

In fact, however, model (4) does not readily accord with a justificationist semantics. The assertion of a mathematical statement, intuitionistically understood, is a claim, if not on the part of the individual speaker, then on behalf of the mathematical community, to be able to prove the statement, not a prediction that it will at some time be proved. Hence the truth of such an assertion consists of our now having a means of obtaining a proof of the statement, not of our proving it at some time, now or in the future; still less does it consist of there being a proof to be had—something that we could recognize as a proof if we were shown it—even if we never hit on it. If mathematical reality is constituted by the sum total of true mathematical assertions, then mathematical reality continually grows; that is what legitimated Brouwer's introduction, in the theory of the creative subject, of tense into mathematics. Intuitionistically, there can be no statement that is neither true nor false, since, if we have neither proved nor refuted a statement, the possibility is always open that we may at some time do one or the other. But if the question whether we shall ever do the one or the other had a definite present answer, there would be statements that were neither true nor false, those, namely, that we should never either prove or refute.

It appears to follow that, from a justificationist standpoint, empirical reality must likewise constantly change. Not only must the future reveal itself in due time, but to the past itself more must accrue, as we discover new indirect evidence for what happened.

It is, however, unnecessary to regard the future as wholly indeterminate in order to repudiate the idea that, for any given statement, the question whether we shall ever have grounds for asserting it must have a definite present answer: that is to ignore the intuitionist conception of infinity. The question, "Shall we ever have grounds for this statement?" involves the unbounded future, and hence quantification over an infinite totality. But, in intuitionistic logic, it can be assumed that every instance of such a quantification is determinately true or false, without concluding that the same holds good of the quantified statement. We can thus evade the conclusion that there is a trichotomy *eventually verified*, *eventually falsified* and *forever undecided*. Let A(n) be the statement that some decidable state of affairs will obtain, or some observable event occur, on the nth day from now. Then we may consistently hold that, for each n, A(n) determinately either holds good or does not hold good, without thereby supposing that the statement "For some n, A(n)" is determinately either true or false. This is not at all to say that no statement involving quantification over an infinite domain can be true or false; only that the fact that all its instances are true or false does not imply that the same holds good of it.

To see how this can be, we may consider a tree (a Beth tree) showing future possibilities of deciding statements of the form A(n). There are two possibilities for A(1), represented by two nodes below the vertex: the left-hand node represents its truth and the right-hand node its falsity. If it is true, then of course "For some n, A(n)" will be true. If A(1) is false, then there are of course two possibilities for A(2), again represented by two nodes below the right-hand of the two nodes below the vertex (that which represents the falsity of A[1]): A(2) is either true or false. The tree will continue like this all the way down. So long as we remain on the rightmost branch (path), we cannot assert "For some n, A(n)"; but we cannot deny it, either, because there always might be an n for which A(n) held good.

From this it might be argued that a justificationist semantics is committed to the branching future—to the indeterminacy of statements in the future tense. For, if the possibilities represented by the tree which I described are to be *real*, and not merely epistemic, possibilities, then it must be indeterminate, on day n, whether or not $A(n + 1)$. If the possibilities are merely epistemic, it may be supposed that some path in the tree represents the *actual* future, and all that the tree then illustrates is that if, as a matter of fact, there will be no n such that $A(n)$, we shall never know this fact. It does not show that there is no such fact.

This argument fails, because the logical point applies just as well if we reinterpret $A(n)$ as a statement about the past—that some observable event occurred n days *ago*. Although we may assume that, for each n, $A(n)$ is determinately either true or false, we may not infer that the statement "For some n, $A(n)$" is likewise determinately either true or false. Each statement that an observable event took place at a specific time in the past may be definitely true or false, and yet the proposition that such an event ever took place in the past may not be assumed to be so. And yet no one wishes to argue for a branching past: to maintain that an event's having happened at a certain time and its not having happened at that time are both real possibilities.

We should not, in my view, attempt to evade this argument on the score that the past is finite. It seems to me that there is no absolute truth to a statement that the universe has lasted a finite time: it is a matter of calibration—what are counted as equal temporal intervals. If the history of the universe is reckoned to be finite, it can always be recalibrated to make it infinite, and conversely. If we are concerned with the occurrence of events of a certain type, the important question is how long, at any given stage in the history of the universe, it takes such an event to happen.

We ought to accept the charge that the possibilities represented on the tree are epistemic. We should reject the complaint that we were supposed to be concerned with what is true, as opposed to what could be known. The justificationist conception of truth does not oppose them: it explains truth in terms of what is, or can be, or could have been known.

Why should truth be explained in terms of knowledge? The question is whether it is possible to swallow the conception of a reality existing in utter independence of its being apprehended. Could the physical universe have existed quite devoid of sentient creatures? I do not mean to ask whether it could have at some stage have been devoid of sentient creatures—we have good reason to suppose that it was. My question is whether it is intelligible to suppose that the universe might have been devoid of sentient creatures throughout its existence. What would be the difference between the existence of such a universe and there being no universe at all? To express the question theologically, could God have created a universe devoid of sentient creatures throughout its existence? What would be the difference between God's creating such a universe and his merely conceiving of such a universe without bringing it into existence? What difference would its existence make? It seems to me that the existence of a universe from which sentience was perpetually absent is an unintelligible fantasy. What exists is what can be known to exist. What is true is what can be known to be true. Reality is the totality of what can be experienced by sentient creatures and what can be known by intelligent ones.

The fact still remains that the semantics of intuitionistic logic looks toward the future. This is obvious for Beth trees and Kripke trees, which deal with successive states of information, in which we acquire (or may acquire) new information at each stage, but do not lose any. It also applies to the Heyting semantics for mathematical statements in terms of proofs: at later times, new proofs are available to us, and there are therefore new statements we can recognize as true. Suppose that $A(N)$ says that a certain observable event has occurred, or will occur, in the year N A.D. Obviously, the fact that we know that the event has never yet occurred does not tell us whether it ever will; so at present there is, from the standpoint of intuitionistic logic, no truth of the matter whether it ever will or not. If, for some $N \geq 2003$, the event occurs in the year N A.D., there will then of course be a truth of the matter; until then, if ever, there will not. Since at the end of every year, it can be decided whether the event took place in that year, we may elect to hold that either $A(N)$ or $\neg A(N)$ is true for every particular N, although we do not know which. In this case, if, for some $N \geq 2003$, the event is going to occur in the year N A.D., there is now a truth of the matter whether it is ever going to occur. If we choose in this way to represent the future as determinate (in respect of this type of event), we must take care to distinguish between what is now true and what we now know to be true. If for some particular $N \geq 2003$, $A(N)$, then "$\exists N\, A(N)$" is now true; but we do not yet know whether it is true, and shall not know until the year N A.D.

Suppose that we were now to know, for every N, whether $A(N)$ or not: should we then not know whether the event was ever going to occur? Well, what is it to know something? For us, it is certainly not to have it in mind: for one of us to be truly said, at any time, to know his own telephone number, is not to have it continuously in mind but to be able to bring it to mind whenever it is needed. So to know, for every N, whether $A(N)$ or not is to be able correctly to tell, for each N, whether $A(N)$ or not. This ability would in no way help us to answer the question, "Is there an N for which $A(N)$?", unless we happened to ask ourselves whether $A(N)$ held good for some N for which in fact it did. Otherwise we should be no better off than we should be at any time at which the event had not happened yet. For—unless indeed the future is finite—we cannot review every year in turn to discover whether the event was going to take place in that year, for the task is infinite. Of course, the time might come when we discovered a reason why the event could never occur, and then we should know that it never would. But the mere knowledge, for each year, whether the event would occur in that year, could not, by itself, enable us to say whether it ever would. We cannot carry out an infinitary operation, because we can never establish its infinite base.

Must not one who believes in God accept that the future is wholly determinate, since God foreknows how it will be? Realists sometimes appeal to divine omniscience to defend the principle of bivalence, and thereby the determinateness of reality. At first sight, the existence of an omniscient being can have no bearing on what truths there are (other than that of the proposition that there is such a being). Whatever truths there are, God will know them; if there are no truths of a certain kind, he will not know any such. If there are gaps in reality—questions that have no true answer—God will not know any answers to those questions: he knows all that there is to know, but no more than that.

This argument overlooks the self-reflexive character of knowledge. If God knows something, he also knows that he knows it; if he does not know something, he also knows that he does not know it, and hence that it is not true. To object to the "also" on the ground that a truth's holding good and God's knowing it are the very same thing would be irrelevant. What is relevant is that God must know *whether* he knows that such-and-such a thing is so. From this it may appear that omniscience implies bivalence: if God does not know, of some proposition, that it is true, he knows that it is *not* true. Thus it seems that classical logic is the logic of divine thought. But for us to use classical logic is to behave as if we were gods. Is this a correct assessment?

God's foreknowledge is conventionally explained in one of two ways. One is that God's knowledge of how things will be rests on his intention to make them happen so. This explanation implies that God brings about all that happens, and thus restricts our moral freedom to giving our will to it or withholding our will from it; if the same explanation is given of God's foreknowledge of which we shall do, we have no freedom at all. An alternative account is that God apprehends the past, the present, and the future all at once, being himself unchanging. If this were so, he would not apprehend change as it is: only one who is in time can be aware of anything *as* changing. The only correct account can be that God simply has (complete) foreknowledge, just as we have (incomplete) memory.

Since it does not conflict with justificationism to suppose that it is now true, of any observable event, that it will take place at any specific time, or that it will not, no problem arises about attributing knowledge of such truths to God. God's knowledge cannot be like ours, however—a potentiality to tell the answer to a question when that question comes up. An infinite mind must, rather, be continuously aware of all the knowledge it possesses; and therefore God must know, for any event, whether or not he knows of a time when it will occur; if he does not, then it will never occur.

Having everything one knows simultaneously in mind lies far from our capacity to imagine; but we cannot here appeal to God's thoughts being beyond our comprehension, as undoubtedly many of them are. The thought that some observable event will never occur is well within our comprehension. We cannot judge such a thought true unless we have some reason to hold that there is some obstacle to such an event's ever occurring; but that God could know it true by scanning all future time is sufficiently like our method of establishing generalizations about finite totalities to serve as a verification of the thought as we understand it.

The deduction of bivalence from omniscience is fallacious. A proposition is true if there are grounds to be had for it, whether or not we are in possession of them. It is false if its negation is true, that is, if there is an obstacle to there ever being grounds for it. That is why there can be gaps in reality; the absence of such an obstacle does not entail that there *are* any grounds for the proposition. If there is such a gap, God does not know either the truth or the falsity of the proposition in question. It follows that the proposition fails to be true, but not that its negation, as we understand negation, holds good. Bivalence does not follow from God's knowing every truth. A proposition may fail to be true in two cases: its being false and there being a truth-value gap. But we cannot give this sense to "not true," since we cannot recognize any specific gap in reality. Indeed, we cannot even consistently envisage there being any such gap in a particular case; this would be to envisage a proposition's being neither true nor false, and this would be a contradictory supposition. We may rightly declare a proposition to be false only when God knows it to be false, that is, when we recognize an obstacle to its being true. This is the sense of "false" to which we appeal when we say that God does not know a given proposition to be false; we cannot consistently extend the term to cover cases when there is no truth of the matter. Justificationist semantics requires us to use intuitionistic logic. It can never be ruled out that we may find grounds for any proposition that we have not recognized as being false. We may sometimes be able to recognize that some proposition cannot be false without yet being able to pronounce it true; but we cannot ever determine it not to be true.

God can know where a gap in reality occurs, by knowing neither the truth nor the falsity of some proposition; he has available to him a negation which is not available to us. It might therefore be urged that the logic of God's thought, a logic to whose application we cannot attain, is a three-valued, rather than a classical, one.

These last speculations turn on difficult theological questions, and I make no claim to be good at theology; perhaps theologians, even if sympathetic to justificationism, will spurn my speculations. They are of no interest to those who have no belief in God. Realists have sometimes argued for bivalence from the mere *conception* of an omniscient being; but such an argument could be founded only on his actual existence. One cannot argue to how things *are* from how they *would be* in circumstances one believes not to obtain.

6

TRUTH: DENIERS AND DEFENDERS

Very early in his book, *Truth and Truthfulness: An Essay in Genealogy* (Princeton and Oxford: Princeton University Press, 2002, pp. 4–5), Bernard Williams speaks of those philosophers whom he calls "deniers" of truth. He characterizes them very broadly, as adopting "a style of thought that extravagantly, challengingly or . . . irresponsibly denies the possibility of truth altogether, waves its importance aside, or claims that all truth is 'relative' or suffers from some other such disadvantage." They are, he says, "disposed to dismiss the idea of truth as the object of our inquiries altogether, or to suggest that if truth is supposed to be the object of inquiry, then there is no such thing and that what passes itself off as inquiry is really something else." It is not until much later in the book (p. 59) that one of these deniers is for the first time identified, as Richard Rorty. On p. 128 we learn that Rorty's principal qualification for this status is that he denies that truth is the goal of inquiry. Williams gives a somewhat woolly account of what, for Rorty, the goal of inquiry is: "some psychological or social state, which we may call 'being justified in believing that P' or 'our all being in reasonable agreement that P'." Now what Rorty actually says is this (in "Is Truth a Goal of Inquiry? Donald Davidson versus Crispin Wright," *Philosophical Quarterly* 45 [July 1955]: 281–300, repr. in *Philosophical Papers, Vol. 3: Truth and Progress* [Cambridge: Cambridge University Press, 1998], pp. 19–42):

> Pragmatists think that if something makes no difference to practice, it should make no difference to philosophy. This conviction makes them suspicious of the distinction between justification and truth, for that difference makes no difference to my decisions about what to do. If I have concrete, specific doubts about whether one of my beliefs is true, I can resolve those doubts only by asking whether it is adequately justified—by finding and assessing additional reasons pro and con. I cannot bypass justification and confine my attention to truth: assessment of truth and assessment of justification are, when the question is about what I should believe now, the same activity. This line of thought suggests to pragmatists that, although there is obviously a lot to be said about justification of various sorts of beliefs, there may be little to say about truth. (p. 19)

There is nothing here about psychological or social states, merely a notion, not further explained, of a belief's being justified. The argument can apply only to those who think that a belief's being justified makes it more likely to be true; for anyone who does not think this, the assessment of truth and the assessment of justification cannot be at all the same activity. But what is established by the argument? Certainly not that there is little to say about truth. If one is suspicious of the distinction between justification and truth, one must think, or at least suspect, that if there is a great deal to say about justification, there must be a great deal to say about truth. The passage strongly suggests the conclusion that, at least when we are concerned with the goal of inquiry, we should simply jettison the notion of truth and employ only that of justification.

If this *is* Rorty's conclusion, we must ask how far he thinks it can be generalized: can we omit the restrictive clause "when we are concerned with the goal of inquiry"? Can we jettison the notion of truth altogether? If so, then Rorty can indeed properly be said to be a denier.

Williams does not believe that Rorty, by appealing to the notion of justification, has dispensed with that of truth. He says:

> If the social or psychological states in question are called such things as "being justified in believing that P" or "our being in reasonable agreement that P", . . . these descriptions already call on the notion of truth. A justified belief is one that is arrived at by a method, or supported by considerations, that favour it, not simply by making it more appealing or whatever, but in the specific sense of giving reason to think that it is true. (p. 129)

If someone said that the goal of following a certain diet recommended by the dieticians was not best described as being to achieve a healthy diet, but as being to comply with the recommendations of the dieticians, it could be replied that the dieticians recommended their diet *as a healthy one*. Does Williams refute Rorty when he argues similarly about justification and truth? No. We do not have any general practice of eating as the dieticians recommend that we should eat; anyone must give a reason for following their recommendations, and this reason must invoke the concept of a healthy diet. But we do have an accepted practice of justifying our beliefs and assertions: we use certain forms of argument, adduce certain kinds of evidence—in short, engage in all that would be comprised in that account to which Rorty alludes of the justification of various sorts of beliefs. It is far from obvious that, in order to acquire, or even to see the point of, this complex of practices, we have to appeal to the concept of truth.

Doubtless, in order to *justify* our practices of justification, we should have to invoke the concept of truth. Williams does believe that such justification is in place: there is room for an account of why certain methods of inquiry are what he calls "truth-acquiring," and others are not. Rorty does not think that any such account is called for: he commends Donald Davidson (p. 24) for having no sympathy with the idea that philosophers can "under-write our assumption that, the more justification we can offer of a belief, the likelier it is that that belief is true."

Suppose it said that a chess player does not aim to adopt a winning strategy, but only to adopt a strategy that promises to be a winning one: that, after all, is the type of strategy that he does adopt. The remark would be obviously fatuous, and would be open to an objection parallel to Williams's objection to Rorty. What shows that the chess player's object is indeed to follow a winning strategy is that, if he loses a game by following some apparently promising strategy, he will in the future abandon or modify that strategy. Rorty appears to concede that an inquirer will act in a precisely analogous way. He defends the contrast expressed by what he calls the "cautionary" use of "true" (*Philosophical Papers, Vol. 1: Objectivity, Relativism and Truth* [Cambridge: Cambridge University Press, 1991], p. 128): by saying, "It was justified but it was not true", one may be indicating that one is appealing to a different audience than that by whose lights the assertion was justified. He insists that justification is relative to the audience addressed (*Truth and Progress*, p. 4), and that a new audience may have different standards of justification from an old one.

Presumably we are not intended to read this as advocating the crassest relativism, recommending us to assert whatever our hearers are disposed to find credible; Rorty is anxious to fend off the accusation of relativism. Rather, we must suppose that the standards of the new audience are sounder than those of the old, and for that reason will be adopted by the speaker; in *Truth and Progress* Rorty speaks of a "better" audience (p. 22). But then we learn that it is impossible to show that our methods of inquiry conduce to the discovery of the truth. Thus Rorty says, "I deny [Michael] Williams's claim that 'it is surely an essential feature of epistemic justification that justifying a belief makes it more likely to be true'" (*Truth and Progress*, p. 24, fn. 21). It must follow from this that we can never claim to have adopted objectively better standards of justification, ones that bring us closer to the truth: one audience may be better informed or more imaginative than another, but we cannot claim that its standards of justification are better, or that what is justified by its standards is more likely to be true than what is justified by the standards of the "worse" audience. We cannot claim to have made progress by some objective criterion; all we can say is that we have made progress *by our lights*.

This familiar move takes us back to relativism. Unless our changing standards of justification really do provide us with a higher chance of attaining the truth, all there are are *different* standards, to which it will be advisable to conform when addressing one audience or another.

Rorty remarks in the footnote cited above that he enlarged on his denial that justification of a proposition makes its truth more probable in his article "Sind Aussagen universelle Geltungsansprüche?" (*Deutsche Zeitschrift für Philosophie* 42 [6] [1995]: 975–88). We saw that Rorty's claim that the assessment of truth and the assessment of justification are the same activity can apply only to those who hold the belief he here declares to be illusory. His denial is certainly paradoxical. Justification of a proposition may include evidence for it, or a compelling argument for it. So, according to Rorty, our having evidence in favor of the proposition "The universe is expanding" does not make its truth more probable than if we had no evidence either way. Rorty allows the disquotational use of "true" as one use of the word, so he is committed to the view that our having evidence that the universe is expanding does not make it more probable that the universe is expanding than if we had none.

In his German article, following his frequent practice of presenting his views as interpretations of Davidson, Rorty argues as follows:

> For Davidson truth is not a goal. It cannot be a goal, because we have no capacity to recognise it whenever we find it. If we are to fix on a goal common to every disputation, it must simply be agreement, which, like justification, is never universal and absolute, but always localised and relative. Justification is always justification *to* someone in particular, whereas truth is never truth for any specific individual. Davidson happily admits that truth is never relative to anything whatever, but he would not admit that a statement automatically calls upon universal validity. For him justification is only a relative, epistemic concept, and truth a non-relative, semantic one. Nothing connects the two concepts. (p. 977)

The thesis that there is no connection between justification and truth certainly implies that justification does not make truth more probable; but it contradicts the proposition that assessment of truth and assessment of justification are the same activity. However, the argument for so strong a conclusion is feeble indeed. We can often be sure that we are in possession of the truth about some matter; but the fact that, in problematic cases, we cannot be sure whether we have reached our goal does not show that it was not our goal. That one concept is relative and epistemic and another absolute and semantic does not prove that there is no connection between them; a similar relation obtains between the concept of inferring one proposition from another and that of the second's implying the first, yet there is an evident connection between them.

Rorty does not offer us a coherent position. He repudiates relativism and sketches a defense against it. Yet he demolishes this defense. His negative theses lead inexorably to relativism. He is not advancing a defensible version of pragmatism: he is simply in a muddle.

Williams does believe that we can demonstrate that our methods of inquiry conduce to our arriving at the truth. His discussion of the matter is, however, somewhat disappointing. The question seems, he says, to require an answer that is at once general and substantial. The appearance is misleading: the level at which the account has to be substantive is not the same as that at which it has to be general. The explanation why a particular method of inquiry is efficacious in arriving at the truth depends on the particular content of the topic being inquired into, and this is a problem for epistemology, which is not the branch of philosophical investigation with which Williams is concerned in the book. But, although general propositions about the truth-acquiring capabilities of our methods of inquiry can be formulated, they are largely trivial or uninteresting. It appears that problems at this general level will also have to be handled by epistemologists.

Williams therefore diverts his attention to a question more germane to the topic of his book: "granted that there are methods of inquiry that are, for different kinds of proposition, truth-acquiring, what are the qualities of people who can be expected to use such methods reliably?" (p. 133). The question is not germane to *our* topic in the present essay. It leads Williams, however, to a discussion of wishful thinking and its avoidance; this prompts him to remark that to repudiate wishful thinking may be thought to imply "not just an idea of truth but a specifically *realist* idea of truth, in the sense of an independent order of things to which our thought is answerable" (p. 136). Williams asks how far such a realistic conception arises from our experience of reality's resistance to the will: things do not turn out as we wish them to. Indeed, we may add that they often surprise us, even when we had no particular wish concerning how they would be. But Williams rejects the idea that this is the source of realism. Mathematical facts frequently turn out not to be as we should have liked them, but we do not therefore need to conclude that our mathematical beliefs are "answerable to an order of things that exists independently of our thoughts" (p. 137).

Here, although he does not see it in precisely that way, Williams is drawing a genuine distinction between two different understandings of the notion of realism. On one understanding, it consists of the truth of propositions being independent of our will; it is realism in that sense that is forced upon us by our experience of the world's resistance to our will. But a different understanding of realism is relevant to realism about mathematics. Realism in this sense consists in the truth of propositions being independent of our knowledge and our capacity for knowledge. The adherent of realism about mathematical reality—the platonist, as he is conventionally called—believes that a mathematical proposition may be true independently of whether we know it or can know it; for him, any well-defined mathematical proposition must be determinately either true or false independently of whether we have or ever shall have any means of recognizing it as true or as false. For his opponent, the constructivist, the only conception of truth we can legitimately claim to have for mathematical propositions is one that equates their truth with our capacity to prove them.

Realism in this latter sense obviously has little to do with the resistance of truth, as we discover it, to our will, though doubtless our infantile experience of this helps to form in us a realistic conception of the world long before we are capable of distinguishing one understanding of realism from the other. Williams's explanation of why the fact that mathematical truth is not subject to our will is not decisive in favor of realism about mathematics is different: he thinks that the decisive feature is our ability to conceive of an intelligible alternative to a state of affairs we have discovered to obtain. In the mathematical case, there is no conceivable alternative; in the empirical case, there is. This, according to Williams, is what underpins realism about empirical matters, but it has no bearing on realism about mathematics. To whatever understanding of realism the possibility of a conceivable alternative may be relevant, it is plainly *not* relevant to the second of the two conceptions of realism I distinguished above, since it is to what we have discovered to be the true state of affairs that the conceivable but not actual state of affairs is an alternative. This notion has to do with what we have discovered to be true: realism, on the second understanding of it characterized above, has to do with what we have *not* discovered, and may never be in a position to discover, to be true.

Williams and Rorty share one thing in common, however: they both believe truth to be indefinable, as Frege did. Rorty forswears a "pragmatist theory of truth" (*Objectivity, Relativism and Truth*, p. 127); for him, the pragmatist wishes to dissolve "the traditional problematic about truth," not to solve it. The problem is dissolved when we observe that the word "true" has just three uses: (a) to endorse what someone else says, as in "Yes, that's quite true"; (b) to caution, as in "Your belief is justified, but perhaps not true"; and (c) to effect disquotation in metalinguistic remarks. This technique of explaining the meaning of a word by listing types of occasion on which it would be used is reminiscent of that of Oxford "ordinary language" philosophers, but the listing seems very haphazard—there are many utterances of "true" it would be difficult to fit into the classification. The crucial question is the relation among the different uses. If after some observation of Brown's, Jones says, "Yes, that's true," while Robinson says,

"That is justified, but not true," is Robinson contradicting Jones? Or are there occasions when it would be correct to make either comment, as there are occasions when it is correct to say either "That's a duck" or "That's not a duck, it's a drake"? Rorty remarks in a footnote that "there is much to be said about the relations between these three uses" of the word "true," but that he is not going to say it in this place; he merely alludes to Robert Brandom's article "Pragmatism, Phenomenalism and Truth Talk" (*Midwest Studies in Philosophy* 12 [1988]: 75–94) as the best attempt at doing so he knows. In fact, Brandom notes the obvious relation of the disquotational or prosentential way of construing "true" to the endorsement "That's true," but says nothing about Rorty's alleged cautionary use of "true." Rorty seems to be unaware that without an explanation of the relations among all three uses, we do not know what his account of the meaning of "true" is. His remark in *Truth and Progress*, p. 25, fn. 23, that "there is no deep reason why 'true' is used to do both of these jobs"—the jobs in question being "to designate what is preserved by valid inference" and "to caution people that beliefs justified to us may not be justified to other, better audiences"—suggests that he thinks that there need be no conflict between Jones and Robinson.

Williams quotes Davidson as calling truth indefinable in his Dewey lectures on "The Structure and Content of Truth." On a strict understanding of "definition," the thesis that truth is indefinable is doubtless correct: but indefinability is not to be confused with inexplicability. It is not to be conceived that, for any of our concepts, it is impossible to give an account of how we acquire it and of what our possession of it consists, when we have acquired it. It is particularly contrary to reason to conceive this concerning such a concept as that of truth, one of an abstract character yet with multiple connections to other concepts. Williams does stress these connections, and he usefully explores the relation between the concepts of truth and of assertion; their connection is indeed of prime importance.

Yet what Williams writes on the matter comes nowhere near what is required to elucidate the concept of truth—an explanation of how we do or can acquire the concept, and an account of that in which our possession of that concept consists; still less does what Rorty writes on the matter. Such an elucidation is possible only when an explanation of the concept of truth is embedded in an explanation of the concept of meaning. Williams and Rorty both make the same far-reaching philosophical mistake, to discuss the concept of truth otherwise than in the context of a discussion of the concept of meaning.

As I have stressed in numerous writings, the concepts of truth and meaning cannot be explained separately; only *together* can they be illuminatingly explained. The fault common to the classical theories of truth, the correspondence and coherence theories, was that they attempted to explain the concept of truth by taking meanings as given. For they proposed a condition for a *proposition* to be true; and what proposition is expressed by the utterance of a sentence evidently depends upon the meaning of that sentence. This requires that meaning can be explained in advance of truth. On some conceptions of meaning, this is indeed possible. The intuitionist account of the meanings of mathematical statements is that the meaning of such a statement is determined by what is to count as a proof of it. But this does not leave truth to be characterized however we see fit, independently of this account of meaning. Mathematical proof has a close connection with mathematical truth; it is our possession of a proof of a mathematical statement that entitles us to recognize it as true. The intuitionist account of meaning for mathematical statements does not yet dictate what we ought to take the truth of mathematical statements to consist of; but it does require that we should explain it by reference to that notion—the notion of proof—in terms of which the meanings of such statements, according to this theory, are given.

In his early writings, Davidson made the opposite error. By

turning a Tarskian truth-definition on its head to obtain a theory of meaning, he attempted to give the form of such a theory while taking the concept of truth as given. What is the point of sketching a theory of meaning for some particular language? It might be that we choose to take this route to achieving a knowledge of the language: that would be a practical point. But what is the *philosophical* point of sketching such a theory of meaning? Presumably it is to arrive at an understanding of the concept of meaning, or of that of a language. If so, the sketch of the theory would achieve its philosophical purpose only if it were possible to attain the concept of truth before acquiring that of meaning. But how could this be? Truth would have to be conceived initially as attaching to nonlinguistic items—beliefs, perhaps—since to have so much as the concept of linguistic items would be already to possess some concept of meaning; but truth, so understood, would have to be taken as capable of being attached to linguistic utterances, otherwise the theory of meaning could never be formulated. None of this sounds in the least like Davidson. He first sets up his theory of meaning for a language in terms of truth as attaching to statements made in it, and then introduces the concept of belief for speakers of that language. This is because he has taken the notion of truth as *given*, without inquiring how it was given or what it is to grasp it. Directly these inquiries are made, it becomes evident that it cannot be taken as given.

Williams is not, indeed, attempting to explain the notion of truth. He is, however, defending it against its deniers. In doing so, he is taking for granted that we know the meaning of what we say. Moreover, in speaking of "a specifically realist idea of truth," he tacitly acknowledges that there are different conceptions of truth. Such different conceptions of truth depend upon differing conceptions of meaning. It is difficult to defend the notion of truth without making clear what conception of truth one is defending, if not arguing in favor of it. He may therefore be making a mistake similar to that made by the classical theories of truth. Whether or not he is doing so depends on how he thinks the meanings of our words and sentences are given to us; but this he does not say, since he does not discuss the concept of meaning at all. If he thinks it is by determining the conditions for the truth of utterances of the sentences of our language, then he is making the same mistake as the early Davidson.

Rorty, by contrast, *does* seek to explain truth. By his account, the word "true" has three uses: (1) the endorsing use, under which "That's true" means "I say the same"; (2) the cautionary use, under which "Though justified, that may not be true" means "A different audience might not find it justified"; and (3) the disquotational use. Why Rorty does not think that the first use of "true" can be subsumed under the third is obscure. He tells us (*Truth and Progress*, p. 21) that "we pragmatists have often fallen back on minimalism" about truth, "and have suggested that Tarski's breezy disquotationalism may exhaust the topic of truth." The reference to Tarski is skewed. The truth of "T-sentences" of the form " 'May follows April' is true if and only if May follows April" is not part of Tarski's theory of truth; rather, the derivability of all T-sentences relating to the object-language is a criterion for the adequacy of the truth-definition. Some critics of disquotationalism have complained of the lack of an account of the semantic connection between the two clauses of every T-sentence. But a Tarskian truth-definition does not lay down the truth of all such T-sentences. It does not itself employ the notion of a T-sentence. It is simply that every T-sentence will drop out as the consequence of the definition. If Tarski can be called a disquotationalist at all, he is certainly not a breezy one.

Rorty's nuanced deflationist or disquotationalist account of truth—nuanced because it allows that there are two uses of "true" not to be explained disquotationally—precludes his thinking, for all his admiration of Davidson, that meaning is given by determining the truth-conditions of our utterances, any more than Tarski could. Tarski was well aware that he could not do so: in "The Semantic Conception of Truth," he clear-sightedly replied to the objection that the meanings of the sentential operators are given by their truth-tables by denying that they are so given, rather than by a formal system governing them. A recognition of the correctness of the proposition expressed by a T-sentence requires a grasp of the meanings of its two clauses, and hence of the sentence forming one clause and referred to in the other. How Rorty supposes that the meanings of the words and sentences of our language are given to us he does not say: he discusses truth but not meaning. But for him the notion of meaning must be prior to that of truth, as it was for the classical theories of truth. Williams and Rorty make the same fundamental philosophical error, to discuss the concept of truth independently of that of meaning, rather than explaining those two concepts *together*.

The concept of truth cannot be explained disquotationally. It has its role in everyday discourse; but it is also a semantic concept. As such, it is a theoretical notion belonging to a semantic theory, which forms a basic component of a theory of meaning. According to a disquotationalist account of truth, the validity of all T-sentences constitutes all that we need to know in order to grasp the concept. It is frequently said, by those who adhere to this account, that the predicate "true" is not needed when we are speaking of individual statements, only when we attempt general formulations. It is evident, however, that to grasp the content of semantic theses involving truth, even as applied to particular statements, demands more than a knowledge of the validity of all T-sentences. Consider, for example, the principle of bivalence, namely that every well-defined statement is either true or false. The disquotationalist must regard this principle as reducing to the logical law of excluded middle. For him, to say, " 'Zebras are striped' is true" is strictly equivalent to saying, "Zebras are striped"; he holds, analogously, that to say, " 'Zebras are striped' is false" is strictly equivalent to saying, "Zebras are not striped." Hence, for him, to say that "Zebras are striped" is either true or false must be strictly equivalent to saying, "Either zebras are striped or zebras are not striped." But the semantic principle and the logical law are *not* equivalent. Suppose that the color of a certain object is on the borderline between red and orange. Then to point at it and say, "That is either red or orange" is surely to make a true statement; since what is orange is not red, to have said, "That is either red or not red" would likewise have been to make a true statement. But it would be wrong to say, of the statement "That is red," that it was either true or false, since it is incorrect to assert a false statement or the negation of a true one, whereas, applied to a borderline case, neither assertion is incorrect. The same holds good if we imagine a Tarskian truth-definition to be given for the English language: although Tarski termed his definition "the semantic conception of truth," it is precisely the use of the term "true" in semantic theory that it leaves out of account.

"For a given class of propositions, how are the ways of finding out whether they are true related to what it is for them to be true?" Williams asks (pp. 132–33); but he discouragingly replies that "these problems are not the present concern." They are, surely, of pressing concern to anyone trying to explore the concept of truth. There are three problems here mentioned: what it is for a proposition of a given class to be true; in what way we can find out whether it is true; and how these two things are related. We cannot conceivably hope to make any progress in answering any of these questions without some account of how the content of such a proposition is given to us, that is, what it is to grasp the meaning of a sentence that expresses the proposition.

Every theory of meaning must respect the primacy of sentences—the principle enunciated by Frege that the sense of a word or expression that can be a component of a sentence consists in its contribution to the sense of any sentence containing it. Thus, as Wittgenstein observed in *Philosophical Investigations*, the substance of attributing a denotation to a name derives from the use of the name in a sentence to say something about what it denotes. The theory will not of course rest content with a merely programmatic characterization of sense: it will specify, for different types of expression, the type of contribution that they make to the senses of sentences in which they occur, and, for particular expressions of a given type, the particular contributions that they make. But these contributions must always be described *as* contributions: the specifications of their meanings must always gain their substance from the account of the meanings of sentences containing them, in accordance with the composition of those sentences. For this reason, the primary delineation of the general form of a theory of meaning is given by what, in general, it takes the meaning of a sentence to consist in.

A sentence, unlike a subsentential expression (except when the rest is "understood," as in answering a question), can be used to *say* something; and what it says, in the relevant sense of "say," when it is used on its own to make an assertion is its *assertoric content*. This is what a hearer comes to believe if he takes the assertion to be correct. But a sentence may also be used as a component of a more complex sentence: its contribution to the sense of the more complex sentence is its *ingredient sense*. That two sentences, when uttered on their own to make assertions, convey the same information to a hearer shows only that their assertoric contents are the same. It does not show that they have the same sense, for their ingredient senses may differ. Williams observes (p. 64) that it is "widely agreed" that all T-sentences are correct, and that an account of truth should explain this fact; but this wide agreement is misguided. "Vesuvius will erupt soon" and " 'Vesuvius will erupt soon' is true" have the same assertoric content, but it cannot be assumed that they have the same ingredient sense. The T-sentence connecting these two sentences involves their ingredient senses, since they are both subsentences of the T-sentence; it will depend upon the particular theory of meaning we favor, and the semantic theory it incorporates, whether this and other T-sentences are to be recognized as correct or not.

The style of meaning-theory by far the most widely favored among present-day philosophers of language is the classical two-valued truth-conditional variety. In this type of theory of meaning, the meaning of a declarative sentence is determined by the condition for any particular utterance of it to be true. This, according to a truth-conditional theory, serves to determine both its assertoric content and its ingredient sense. Here, then, the relation between truth and meaning is absolutely direct.

A truth-conditional theorist of meaning has by no means done all that is required of him, however, if, having enunciated this direct connection between truth and meaning, he says that truth cannot be defined, but that everyone knows what it is. If a theory of meaning is to serve the purpose of explaining what it is for something to be a language, and hence what, in general, it is for a sequence of sounds or of written or printed marks to possess linguistic meaning, it must incorporate an account of how language functions, that is, of the practice of using the language. If the meanings of sentences of the language have been characterized truth-conditionally, the connection must be made between the conditions for the truth of sentences and the practice of uttering them. The account must comprise a description of what a speaker commits himself to in making an assertion by the utterance of a sentence with a given truth-condition, what responses on the part of his hearers are appropriate or will be evoked, when the speaker is regarded as justified in making his assertion, and so on. All this will be part of the explanation of the notion of truth that underlies the assignment to particular sentences of their specific senses by explaining the conditions for their truth.

Rorty proposes to treat justification rather than truth as the goal of inquiry; Williams rejects this proposal. The question cannot be fruitfully debated until we have decided what our conception of truth is to be. As we saw, by speaking of a specifically realist idea of truth, Williams tacitly acknowledged that there are different conceptions of truth. Different conceptions of truth depend upon differing conceptions of meaning, so the opposition between justification and truth cannot be resolved until we have decided what form our theory of meaning is to take. Truth-conditional theories of meaning are opposed by justificationist ones, which take the notion of justification rather than that of truth as central. What prompts such theories is a thought similar to that of Rorty in concluding that justification is the goal of inquiry: namely that when we acquire the practice of using language, what we learn is what is taken to justify assertions of different types. We learn what is accepted as entitling us to make those assertions; we learn also whether what justifies us in doing so is conclusive or whether it is defeasible, that is, capable of being overthrown by subsequent counterevidence. We do *not* learn what it is for those assertions to be true independently of any means we have for establishing their truth. How could we? If we are not in a position either to assert or to deny a given proposition, we cannot be shown what nevertheless makes it true or false. So, according to a theory of this kind, to grasp the meaning of a statement is to know what would justify asserting it or denying it.

On such a theory, meaning is to be explained in terms of justification, that is, what is agreed to count as justifying the assertion of one or another form of statement. But since our conception of truth is to accord with our model of meaning, the notion of truth appropriate to such a theory of meaning must also be given in terms of justification. Exactly what a justificationist conception of truth should be does not immediately follow from this. We do not need straightforwardly to equate the truth of a statement with the

existence of a justification for asserting it. We may think it better
to take a statement as true if it is or was possible to find a justification of it; and there is plenty of room for seeking to characterize
the relevant notion of possibility. What we cannot do is regard
truth as a property which every statement either determinately
possesses or determinately lacks, independently of whether we ever
have any means of deciding which it does; it was precisely the
repudiation of that classical conception of truth which prompted
our adoption of a justificationist theory of meaning in the first
place. If the meaning of a statement is given in terms of what
would justify an assertion of it, the only conception of its truth
must be given in the same terms.

Rorty has confused the issue by substituting an opposition
between justification as the goal of inquiry and truth as the goal of
inquiry for the opposition between meaning as explained in terms
of conditions for justification and meaning as explained in terms of
conditions for truth. On a justificationist theory of meaning, there
can be no opposition between justification and truth as the aim of
inquiry. They are the *same* goal, because, however truth is to be
explained in such a theory, our actually possessing a justification of
a proposition must always imply, and be the best guarantee of, its
truth. For Williams, it seems, truth and justification are quite distinct: a proposition may be true even though no justification of it
exists or is attainable. Nevertheless, justification constitutes our
ground for regarding a proposition as true: what we recognize as
justifying the assertion of a proposition must follow from what we
take as the condition for it to be true. This, it will be recalled, was
a topic that Williams declined to pursue; it remains that the possibility of showing how what we count as evidence for the truth of
a statement can be derived from what we take as the condition for
its truth is a demand upon truth-conditional theories of meaning
if they are to qualify as fulfilling what is required of a theory of
meaning, namely that it serves to explain our linguistic practice as

a whole. Since justification bears this relation to truth for any viable theory of meaning, Williams remains as entitled as a justificationist to regard truth as being the goal of inquiry. But since he gives so little account of what, in his view, constitutes linguistic meaning, and how it is related both to truth and to evidence, he has done little to vindicate his entitlement. The task of the philosopher is neither to belittle truth nor to exalt it, neither to deny it nor to defend it, but to explain why we need the concept and what it is to possess it.

NOTES

1. THE CONCEPT OF TRUTH

1. Jena: Pohle, 1893–1903. Translated in part as *The Basic Laws of Arithmetic: Exposition of the System*, Montgomery Furth, ed. and trans. (Berkeley: University of California Press, 1964).

2. See Unger, *Ignorance: A Case for Skepticism* (New York: Oxford University Press, 1975), chapter 2; Lewis, "Scorekeeping in a Language Game" (1979), reprinted in *Philosophical Papers*, Vol. I (New York: Oxford University Press, 1983), pp. 233–49, and "Elusive Knowledge" (1996), reprinted in *Papers in Metaphysics and Epistemology* (New York: Cambridge University Press, 1999), pp. 418–45.

3. For example, "Radical Interpretation," in *Inquiries Into Truth and Interpretation* (New York: Oxford University Press, 1984), pp. 125–39.

4. *Logical Investigations*, Dermot Moran, ed., J. N. Findlay, trans. (New York: Routledge, 2001), Volume I, Investigation I, section 10, pp. 193–94.

5. See *Philosophy of Logic* (Englewood Cliffs, N.J.: Prentice-Hall, 1970), p. 12.

6. Given in personal conversation.

2. THE INDISPENSABILITY OF THE CONCEPT OF TRUTH

1. See *Naming and Necessity* (Cambridge, Mass.: Harvard University Press, 1980), p. 48.

2. *Tractatus Logico-Philosophicus*, D. F. Pears and B. F. McGuiness, trans. (New York: Humanities Press, 1961).

3. STATEMENTS ABOUT THE PAST

1. "The Reality of the Past," *Proceedings of the Aristotelian Society*, n.s., 69 (1969): 239–58, reprinted in *Truth and Other Enigmas* (Cambridge, Mass.: Harvard University Press, 1978), pp. 358–74.

4. THE SEMANTICS OF THE PAST TENSE

1. "What is a Theory of Meaning? (II)," in Gareth Evans and John McDowell, eds., *Truth and Meaning: Essays in Semantics* (New York: Oxford University Press, 1976), pp. 67–137; reprinted in *The Seas of Language* (New York: Oxford University Press, 1993); see pp. 46, 60.

5. THE METAPHYSICS OF TIME

1. In his *Scientific Thought* (New York: Harcourt Brace, 1923).
2. See "The Unreality of Time," in his *Philosophical Studies*, S. V. Keeling, ed. (New York: Longmans, 1934), pp. 110–31.

INDEX